HAIKU BEFORE HAIKU

TRANSLATIONS FROM THE ASIAN CLASSICS

Haiku

FROM THE RENGA MASTERS

Before

TO BASHŌ

Haiku

Translated, with an introduction, by

STEVEN D. CARTER

COLUMBIA UNIVERSITY PRESS

NEW YORK

COLUMBIA UNIVERSITY PRESS
Publishers Since 1893
New York   Chichester, West Sussex

Copyright © 2011 Columbia University Press

Library of Congress Cataloging-in-Publication Data
Haiku before haiku: from the Renga masters to Bashō /
translated, with an introduction, by Steven D. Carter
p. cm. — (Translations from the Asian classics)
Includes bibliographical references.
ISBN 978-0-231-15648-6 (cloth : acid-free paper)—
ISBN 978-0-231-15647-9 (pbk. : acid-free paper)—
ISBN 978-0-231-52706-4 (e-book)
1. Haiku—Translations into English. 2. Japanese poetry—1185–1600—
Translations into English. 3. Japanese poetry—Edo period, 1600–1868—
Translations into English. 4. Renga—Translations into English.
I. Carter, Steven D.
PL782.E3H24 2011
895.6'1008—DC22
2010037030

References to Internet Web sites (URLs) were accurate at the time of writing.
Neither the author nor Columbia University Press is responsible for URLs that
may have expired or changed since the manuscript was prepared.

BOOK DESIGN BY VIN DANG

To Benjamin

Contents

Acknowledgments

AS ALWAYS, I thank my wife, Mary, for her support in all my endeavors. My son Benjamin, to whom this book is dedicated, helped me with proofreading at many stages along the way. Also of great assistance in that regard was Jeffrey Knott, a doctoral student in Japanese literature at Stanford University. Two anonymous readers for Columbia University Press made a number of very helpful suggestions, for which I am duly grateful. Irene Pavitt and Jennifer Crewe of Columbia University Press provided valuable assistance in guiding the project to completion.

HAIKU BEFORE HAIKU

Introduction

ABROAD OR IN JAPAN, mention of the word *haiku* brings to mind Matsuo Bashō (1644–1694), the greatest master of that genre. However, the truth is that the *haiku* form—in an earlier incarnation—was already 500 years old when Bashō began his career in the mid-seventeenth century. During those early times, the genre was referred to not as *haiku* but as *hokku* (initiating verse), reflecting its role as the first verse of a linked-verse sequence.

One of our first glimpses into the origins of the genre comes in *Fukuro zōshi* (*Commonplace Book*, 1157), a compendium of comments on Japanese poetic conventions, practices, and lore produced by the poet-scholar Fujiwara no Kiyosuke (1104–1177). At that time, the 31-syllable *uta* form (following the syllabic pattern 5-7-5-7-7) was unchallenged in its dominance of Japanese poetic culture. But Kiyosuke made mention of other genres as well, including a newer form called *renga* (linked verse). What he had in mind, however, was not the full linked-verse sequence of 100 verses (*hyakuin*), which would later gain its own place of prominence in the Japanese canon; instead, he was speaking specifically of *kusari renga*—"strings of verses" of indeterminate length, composed as a verse-capping game.

One of the things that Kiyosuke stipulated about the composition of *kusari renga* was that such a sequence should begin not with the last two lines of a conventional *uta* but with the first three lines—in other words, not with the *shimo no ku* (7-7) but with the *kami no ku* (5-7-5).[1] His statement—which was probably a reflection of current practices, as far as we can know about them—provided a beginning for a tradition that is still thriving.

Kiyosuke made two other indisputably foundational statements when he recommended that the first verse of a sequence not be dashed off too quickly, thus singling out the composition of the *hokku* as an art that demanded special attention and care, and noted that the initiating verse should be a complete, independent scene or statement.[2] About fifty years later, Emperor Juntoku (1197–1242), another prominent poet, made these points more explicit by insisting that the *hokku* "should be composed by the most appropriate person in the group" and then adding that "a first verse should be a complete statement" (*hokku wa iikiru beshi*).[3] In this way, two of the most fundamental "rules" of *hokku* (and later *haiku*) came into being: the beginning verse should be assigned to poets of skill and experience who could produce verses of true excellence, and it should express not a fragment but a complete thought.

Many poets of Emperor Juntoku's generation left *hokku* in the historical record. Examples like the following by Fujiwara no Tameie (1198–1275), however, suggest that first verses of that time were often strictly occasional in nature—that is, valedictions or declamations at social gatherings rather than independent "works of art." As such, they could memorialize a host of different events—everything from births to deaths to political successes to even impending battles, not to mention *renga* gatherings themselves:

> *Composed as* hokku *for all ten 100-verse sequences of a 1000-verse sequence held at his Chū'in Estate in Saga*

> A brocade?
> That is the look of Saga
> in autumn.[4]

By this time, the standard 100-verse sequence had been established as the formal vehicle of the genre. That only Tameie's *hokku* and not the rest of the sequence was preserved is therefore evidence that full texts were considered ephemera at that time and that even *hokku* were valued primarily as mementos of important social occasions—as something "to be noted for later generations," as Tameie is reported to have said.[5] This pattern was true for the entire thirteenth century, from which no complete text of a *hyakuin* has survived.

The status of linked verse appears not to have changed much in the generation of Tameie's son and heir, Tameuji (1222–1286), who was likewise asked for a verse for a social occasion, this one sponsored by a cleric son:

> In the Fifth Month of 1279, Dharma Eye Jō'i requested a number of people to write 100-verse sequences to present as an offering to Hie Shrine. Tameuji was asked to provide a hokku that would serve for all the sequences.

> Not a single call,
> and already I'm distressed—
> cuckoo![6]

A later poet would report that Tameuji considered himself a true expert at linked verse.[7] What that must have meant at the time, however, was that he was talented at coming up with a verse appropriate to the occasion. Expressing frustration over waiting for the cuckoo's first call was no more unconventional than comparing autumn colors to brocade. Both Tameie and Tameuji were serious and formidable poets in the *uta* form, but neither seems to have paid *hokku* the same kind of artistic attention.

Such dismissive attitudes toward *renga* were still common in the next century as well, as is apparent from an anecdote concerning Reizei Tamesuke (1263–1328)—known as the Fujigayatsu Middle Counselor in reference to his dwelling in that area of Kamakura—and one of his sons:

> Long ago, when the Fujigayatsu Middle Counselor, Lord Tamesuke, was participating in a *renga* gathering, his son, Guards Captain Tamenari, produced an especially interesting verse. After the meeting, Tamesuke gave his son a thorough scolding. "Don't you know enough to store away good ideas to use later in your *uta*?" he said. "For *renga* gatherings, anything that will please the group a little will do."[8]

By this time, however, *renga* had at least gained greatly in popularity, and not only among courtiers. Records tell us that each spring, at temples such as Bishamondō and Hōshōji and in the Washio area of the Eastern Hills of Kyoto, large numbers of *renga* enthusiasts of all social classes would gather for marathon linking sessions. To the extent that such events were truly supervised at all, that service was rendered by *hana no moto rengashi* (Masters of *Renga* Beneath the Blossoms), who were often low-level priests of some of the newer Buddhist sects of the day (the Time sect, the Pure Land sect, and so on). We know much less about the kind of *renga* composed in these settings than we would like, and the information we do have about them is often tinged with the kind of elitist attitudes displayed by Yoshida no Kenkō (ca. 1283–ca. 1352) when he refers to *hana no moto renga* in *Tsurezuregusa* (*Essays in Idleness*, 1329–1333):

> Only a rustic shows his admiration with no restraint. When he goes to see the cherry blossoms, he works his way forward through the throng, his eyes so fixed on the blossoms that he has not a glance for those he pushes aside; then he drinks his rice wine, composes some linked verse, and departs, thoughtlessly breaking off a big branch to take home with him.[9]

From the point of view of an aristocrat and major *uta* poet, commoner enthusiasts seemed to be composing linked verse beneath the blossoms in the same spirit that they shared *saké*—as a social activity. One primary explanation for why we do not have more information about such events is that poems composed at such picnics—even *hokku*—were still considered quite literally blossoms on the wind.

Another reason for the dearth of textual evidence for such popular events, however, is that by the mid-fourteenth century, some court aristocrats were attempting to "elevate" the form artistically and socially, which inevitably involved distancing it from its recent past. The most prominent of these boosters was Nijō Yoshimoto (1320–1388), a high-ranking courtier who, assisted by a *renga* master named Gusai (d. 1376), compiled the first large anthology of linked verse—*Tsukubashū* (*Tsukuba Collection*, 1356)—and a number of treatises and handbooks. Needless to say, such a commitment was based on a high opinion of *renga*—an opinion that forms the substance of another anecdote involving a poet of the Reizei lineage, Tamehide (d. 1372), another son of Tamesuke:

> Once Tamehide called on Yoshimoto. "Kon'a has gotten interested in linked verse. I wonder what will become of his *uta*?" he asked.
>
> Yoshimoto replied, "He is one who from early on has understood the distinctions between *uta* and *renga*. There is really no difference, after all."[10]

Here the condescending attitude of the heir of the Reizei house—understandable, given that the Reizei were specialists in the *uta* form at court—is again apparent. But Yoshimoto's rejoinder is equally clear. While recognizing that there are practical distinctions to be made between *uta* and *renga*—mostly involving the "linking" process that is so central to the nature of the latter—he insists that, in the words related by another student, at bottom "the two are one and the same Way."[11]

It was in the time of Yoshimoto and Gusai that conventions and lore, including those involving the *hokku*, took on the shape that they would retain far into the future. Prefaces to extant *hokku* and other sources indicate that both men knew firsthand about initiating verses composed for *hana no moto renga*; indeed, they included some verses by masters of that sphere in their own collections and writings. Often, however, they appear to have dressed up the verses to suit aristocratic tastes.

This is not to say that with the advent of Yoshimoto, linked verse ceased to be a social form, however. The genre was still composed in groups, after all, and social exchange would always remain a feature of the *renga* aesthetic. Indeed, even the *renga* poets we think of as most skilled and imaginative were obliged by circumstances to produce *hokku* that were largely decorative in effect, as is apparent from two examples by Yoshimoto and Gusai that appear next to each other in *Tsukubashū*:

> *Composed on a moonlit night, when the Prince of the Second Rank was about to leave to see the garden at Urin'in Temple*
>
> In the garden, we see
> the meadows and mountains
> of the moon.[12]

Composed in 1353 for a 100-poem session held at a farewell party for Dōyo when he was leaving for Harima Province

Clouds depart,
winds fade away.
Then autumn rain.[13]

The first of these poems, composed by Yoshimoto, is a panegyric to the poet's host, an imperial prince known as Son'in (1306–1359), proffered in the form of praise for the unearthly beauty of his garden in moonlight, whereas the second, by Gusai, compares the feeling of parting from a friend and patron—the warrior Sasaki Dōyo (1306–1373)—to the dull atmosphere of rainfall after the first excitement of a storm has passed. Both poems are about parting, and both were, when written, as occasional in nature as those by Tameie and Tameuji, if not as clichéd in terms of imagery and conception.

In other words, whether explicitly linked to a social occasion or not, these initiating verses—especially Gusai's—also fit well into the tradition of courtly aesthetics in their vocabulary, conception, and tone. Yoshimoto, even when his own *hokku* failed to go beyond the demands of a specific setting, was adamant about treating *renga* not as a pastime but as a legitimate genre within the larger tradition of *uta*. It was this attitude that would be embraced by the greatest of the *renga* masters who succeeded him—Shinkei (1406–1475), Sōgi (1421–1502), and Sōseki (1474–1533)—and their poetic progeny, whose poetics saw no need to separate the social from the aesthetic.

For Yoshimoto, the endeavor to elevate *renga* to a higher aesthetic sphere demanded focus on the *hokku*, in particular—the proper composition of which he deemed essential to the success of a sequence, socially and artistically:

The first verse is of paramount importance. Nothing too ordinary will produce the right effect. The best *hokku* have a venerable air, and those that do not, usually seem too pedestrian. Past masters thought of the *hokku* as a matter of utmost importance; so much more so should we in these latter days....

A poor first verse can mar the effect of a whole 100-verse sequence. Rather than just tossing something off, then, it is best to leave composition of the *hokku* to a poet of experience and skill.[14]

What sort of verse did Yoshimoto endorse? Even some from earlier times, it would seem—a rhetorical move required in order to claim for *renga* its proper status within the larger discourse of Japanese court poetry. In one of his most important treatises, for instance, Yoshimoto chose an example by Tamesuke, whose rather low opinion of linked verse evidently did not keep him from producing something for which Yoshimoto could express praise, noting that "even if produced yesterday"[15] the poem would be interesting:

Frost melts—
drenching fallen leaves
in sunlight.[16]

Yoshimoto said nothing about where, when, or under what conditions this *hokku* was composed—an act of critical concealment by which he could encourage readers to judge the verse first of all as an object of aesthetic attention. And if we follow Yoshimoto's lead, we discover that the verse is indeed more multi-layered than are most occasional pieces: a winter scene shows the sun melting frost on the trees, producing rain that drips onto fallen leaves that, in turn, sparkle in the cascading light. The word *nururu* is meant both literally, in reference to the "drenching" rainfall from the trees, and figuratively, in reference to the sunlight that "drenches" fallen leaves. The poem thus presents not just a case of confusion of the senses, or simply of metaphor, but also a novel double entendre that joins opposites—above and below, trees and ground, sunlight and rain, warm and cold—in a single realistic yet still elegant scene.

Although we know from various sources that *renga* meetings were not always free from levity or from verses that might have evoked criticism from aristocratic readers, it is true that Yoshimoto's efforts did prevail, at least among the elite.[17] A grand 10,000-verse meeting held at the Kitano Shrine in 1433, for example, may seem to have resembled *hana no moto renga*—which continued to take place, but were effectively marginalized over time—in that it was a large event held in the spring. In every other way, though, the gathering was orchestrated to be courtly and dignified. First of all, it was explicitly modeled not on any *hana no moto* precedent but on a court-sponsored event from 1391, also held at Kitano. What's more, rather than beneath the blossoms, the assembled poets met in various venues within the shrine complex, where strict rules of rank applied in seating and courtly etiquette. Finally, the participants formally included the shogun, numerous court nobles, high-ranking clerics, and *renga* masters of higher pedigree. A record of the gathering written by a former regent traces the origins of the form back to accounts of poem exchanges in the earliest Japanese chronicles, reinforcing the claims made by Yoshimoto. And, significantly, the record preserves the *hokku* and the second and third verses of all 100 sequences.[18]

By the turn of the fifteenth century, then, linked verse and, by extension, the *hokku* form were in the mainstream of elite artistic discourse. While he was doubtless aware of less "serious" work that continued to be produced on the margins of literary culture, it would be the works of this mainstream that later inspired Bashō to say, "The *waka* of Saigyō, the *renga* of Sōgi, the paintings of Sesshū, the tea of Rikyū—the thing that runs through all of these is one and the same."[19] Needless to say, the aesthetic that united these artists—none of whom was in any way a marginal figure—was one facet of the poetic past that Bashō wanted to incorporate into the style that he hoped to establish for his own time and the future.

The history of linked verse after Yoshimoto is therefore a tale of poets working at the very center of elite Japanese literary culture, along with their sometimes less prestigious students and hangers-on. In many ways, it is a history that parallels rather closely what was going on in the world of the older *uta*—not surprisingly, since many *renga* masters composed *uta* and even taught the basics of *uta* composition, especially when traveling through the provinces. One difference between the institutions of *uta* and *renga*, however, was that the latter was not so dominated by old court lineages that had a virtual monopoly on the highest levels of instruction and administration. Rather than bloodline, the world of *renga* revolved around relationships between masters—almost none of whom were of courtly lineage—and their patrons and students, who often were one and the same. Not surprisingly, most of the major poets came from commoner origins, although some aristocrats did participate in *renga* culture.

One does not need further knowledge of *renga* history in all its detail to appreciate the *hokku* of poets who preceded Bashō. But before approaching the works of these early practitioners of the form, answers to three inevitable questions are required. The first is when—if ever—the *hokku* as a subgenre broke free from its identity as the first verse of a full *renga* sequence. The best answer is that it never did, completely, certainly not in the period of time covered by this book. Although there is abundant evidence that *hokku* were sometimes composed by prominent poets—masters such as Sōgi and high-ranking aristocrats such as Sanjōnishi Sanetaka (1455–1537)—who often did not actually participate in the *renga* meetings where those *hokku* were used,[20] it is true that all the *hokku* included in the major anthologies of *renga* until at least the early sixteenth century were originally composed as initiating verses. For that matter, although modern readers do not often realize it, many of Bashō's most famous *hokku* were in fact written as initiating verses for full sequences. One example is a verse from *Oku no hosomichi* (*Narrow Road to the Deep North*, 1694), composed near the Mogami River:

> With mountain cliffs looming left and right, our boat made its descent through lush growth.... The waters of Shiraito Falls were visible here and there through gaps in the greenery. Then came the Hall of Sages, standing before us on the riverbank. Riding such swollen waters, our boat seemed a fragile thing indeed.

> How swift
> the jumble of summer rains:
> Mogami River.[21]

Documents show that this verse, far from being written while the poet was still in the boat, was composed for a 36-verse sequence (*kasen*) held at the home of a certain Ichiei in the town of Ōishida. And this is no isolated example: the same pattern applies to many *hokku* recorded in Bashō's travel records, which, while originating at specific gatherings, were later recontextualized in prose narratives.[22] And there is even more to the story, for manuscript evidence reveals that the *hokku* composed at Ōishida originally read differently:

> How refreshing
> the jumble of summer rains:
> Mogami River.[23]

Why the change? One commentary suggests that the word "refreshing" (*suzushi*) in the original was intended to express Bashō's gratitude to a host who offered respite from life on the road.[24] However one interprets the original, the fact that Bashō later altered the text in order to suit the narrative purposes of *Oku no hosomichi* is undeniable, as is the conclusion that for him the *hokku* was to that extent and in that context, at least, an independent form—a form that was no longer an initiating verse.

Thus the proper reply to the question of when the *hokku* broke free from *renga* must be oblique, identifying a fundamental tension in the genesis of the *hokku* that would continue well into the time of Bashō. The *renga* master Tani Sōboku (d. 1545) expressed it well in a bit of lore passed on to students:

> Should one prepare a *hokku* beforehand, or compose it on the spot?
>
> Because there will be many scenes to choose from around the dwelling and in the room, along with various images in the garden, preparing a *hokku* beforehand is just not feasible. As a rule, then, one must come up with a verse on the spot. However, one can prepare by conceiving something based on the current season and time of year and the surroundings—mountains, rivers, grasses, trees, and so on, and then work in more immediate images on the spot. That is the lore on the subject.[25]

Sōboku must have been aware when he wrote this statement that many *hokku* were in fact prepared beforehand; indeed, sometimes a prominent poet would provide several *hokku* and allow a patron to choose from among them. Nonetheless, he also knew that the primary reason why only experienced poets were asked to compose *hokku* was that doing so demanded special knowledge, competence, and skill, both literary and social, and that most poets should follow his advice literally. As a master of linked verse—and that was his profession—Bashō, too, would have been aware of the tension that Sōboku alluded to between a prepared verse and its final realization in a particular social context. It was in the space created by that tension that *hokku* became more than *hokku* over time.

The second question that must be answered in order to understand the *hokku* translated in this anthology concerns how these early works differ from the poems of Bashō or from modern *haiku*. A less vague answer than that to the first question can be given. Until the modern period, most poets adhered to the basic conventions already enumerated: the *hokku* should be composed by a poet of considerable experience when possible, it should express a complete thought, and it should contain a season word and preferably an allusion to the actual setting of composition—the last requirement being an articulation of the continuing social identity of the form. This is true for the *hokku* in this book, all of which were actually initiating verses composed to begin sequences.

Yet there was one way in which the *hokku* of *renga* poets differed from those of Bashō. For, in keeping with the spirit of Yoshimoto's pronouncements, participants in orthodox meetings—at least until the mid-sixteenth century—continued to eschew the comic, the vulgar, and the colloquial in vocabulary, imagery, theme, and style. In other words, late medieval and early modern *renga* masters still considered themselves to be participants in the *uta* tradition. This is one reason why, when asked how to approach the task of composing a *hokku*, Sōgi went beyond the basic conventions to focus clearly on aesthetics:

> In a *hokku* one must adhere to the season precisely, including nothing discordant but rather employing images such as flowers, birds, the moon, and snow with a mind to producing an effect of dreamy elegance. The syntax of the verse should be normal enough not to invite criticism—although one should experiment by moving words around, from top to bottom or bottom to top.[26]

Bashō would compose many *hokku* on "flowers, birds, the moon, and snow," but he would also compose *hokku* on codfish, fleas, cowsheds, and mud—the latter becoming the sorts of images that readers would in time come almost to expect in what is now universally known as *haiku*. Poets of linked verse, however, continued to produce primarily elegant poems, consigning most of their *iisute* ("toss-away" verses)—a word sometimes used for casual pieces but also for the unpolished, comic, or vulgar verses that they occasionally came up with in linking sessions—to anonymous status. Furthermore, *renga* poets were also committed, at least in a general way, to subordinating their poetic conceptions to the aesthetic ideals of medieval courtly discourse—from *aware* (pathos) and *okashi* (intellectual allure or ingenuity) to *yūgen* (mystery and depth), *ushin* (depth of feeling), and *sabi* (loneliness). Among poets there were individual differences, to be sure—the work of Shinkei (1406–1475) being astringent when compared with the elegance of Sōgi's finest poems, and Inawashiro Kensai (1452–1510) in his richness of conception offering a complement to the cleverness of Satomura Jōha (1524–1602). But especially before the early seventeenth century, those differences may be fairly defined as differences in degree rather than in kind.

The *hokku* that I have translated in this book will in an ironic way, then, offer something new to modern *haiku* enthusiasts—poems that make a clear connection *back* to the traditions of Japanese court poetry while inevitably gesturing *forward* to Bashō, Yosa Buson, Kobayashi Issa, and Masaoka Shiki. For in the sense that *renga*'s initiating verses would in time survive long after *renga* as a genre, to study the *hokku* of Yoshimoto, Sōgi, Jōha, and other early masters of the form may truly be characterized as a way to prepare for reading Bashō, who was more derisive of some of his more immediate forebears than of the great *renga* poets, like Sōgi, of earlier generations.[27]

This leads to the third question, which is intimately related to the previous one. For one way in which *hokku* are like later *haiku* has to do less with aesthetics than with the dynamics of conception—with the primary demands, beyond form and stylistic appropriateness, that informed the creative act of producing the first verse for a sequence, demands that would continue to be important for *haiku* poets as well. The most direct way to approach the matter is to say that the author of a first verse was always presented with a very specific challenge: to compose a verse appropriate to an occasion and to do so in a way that always involved a seasonal reference expressed *as the treatment of an idea,* in much the same way that the author of a traditional *uta* would compose a poem on a conventional topic (*dai*).[28] In some poems, especially those produced for a formal, ritual, or conventional occasion that is specifically described, the impact of this demand is easy to identify. A *hokku* composed by Sōgi at a gathering of friends in a cloister of the great Shōkokuji temple complex in Kyoto provides an example:

> *Composed near a memorial marker to Former Middle Counselor Teika, on the fifteenth day of the Eighth Month*
>
> Day will dawn.
> And shall I ever see again
> such an autumn moon?[29]

Based on the headnote to this *hokku*, one can conclude that those in attendance at the event at Shōkokuji, where Sōgi had studied Zen as a young man, actually had a view of the full moon of mid-autumn, making the verse, on one level, an example of natural description. Obviously, though, Sōgi's conception goes beyond that. For one thing, it entails a direct reference to a famous poem by—who else, given the situation?— Fujiwara no Teika (1162–1241) himself:

> *Written for a 50-poem sequence of "moon" poems, composed at the time when the Go-Kyōgoku Regent was Captain of the Left*
>
> Day will dawn,
> and we will pass beyond
> the mid-point of fall.
> But will the setting moon
> be all that we lament?[30]

Teika's poem was written at a very specific time, midway through the Eighth Month—the time of the full moon, at the midpoint of autumn, season of the moon—and it is time's passing that the rhetorical question of the last two lines is obviously meant to suggest. The full moon must now begin to wane, and autumn must progress into winter; midpoints always signal ends.

To do true honor to his poetic forebear, Sōgi responded to Teika's rhetorical question with one of his own, which was very specifically intended to honor his hosts for the singular experience they had provided for all present on so memorable a night, beneath "such an autumn moon." Thus the hyperbole of the older poem became the foundation for the hyperbole of the newer in a way that makes the latter a true *variation* on a topic—which is exactly what a skilled poet was expected to produce. To complete the effect, one need only note that for Teika, the moon was an important image, as he explained to a student in one of his treatises: "Some time ago . . . when I made a retreat at Sumiyoshi, I had a wonderful dream inspired by the God, in which I was told, 'For you the moon is radiant.'"[31] Sōgi knew that text, of course, and knew that his companions would know it as well. Iconically (and perhaps ironically), his poem briefly reaches back to connect to an earlier time in a place that only seems to be the same, since a memorial tablet can only draw attention to what is no longer there.

Does the many-layered allusive nature of Sōgi's *hokku* mean that we cannot understand it without knowing these background circumstances, allusions, and so forth? The answer is, of course, no. Like all texts, *hokku* survive the demise of the events that produced them, taking on a different life. All the same, knowing the sorts of details given here usually serves to enhance the reading experience and only rarely interferes with other interpretations. Sōgi was involved in a social enterprise, but also a literary one fully as rich as anything that goes by that name in other places and times. What the exercise of exploring the rhetorical complexity of poems like Sōgi's does teach us, however, is that *hokku*, when they were first composed, were seldom straightforward poems of natural description, even when they may easily be understood that way—which was usually true for later *haiku* as well.

Even when we do not know anything about the genesis of a *hokku*, considering the way the topic (usually the season word) is treated is therefore a good place to begin for readers who wish to understand a *hokku* in its immediate context. An example by Kensai, also focusing on the moon, will, I hope, make the point:

No wind at all.
Only light to clear away
clouds from the moon.[32]

In contrast to Sōgi's poem, we know nothing about the circumstances under which this *hokku* was composed. Judging solely on content, the only thing we can assume is that the poem was probably written in autumn, probably on a moonlit night—perhaps on a cloudy, windless night. About one thing, however, we can be more certain: Kensai's primary objective was to produce a memorable poem, even if the actual scene before him was less than memorable. He did so by means of a conception that emphasizes the central feature of the moon—its light, so powerful in his treatment that it can dispense with cloud cover without the help of wind. Once again, the *hokku* does present a landscape, but a dynamic landscape that also expresses an idea. We can therefore surmise that to its original auditors—who must have been present, unless the verse was composed for a solo sequence—the poem represented at least that much, and that any other significance of a more immediate nature that it might have had would not have fundamentally contradicted this most basic of interpretations. However descriptive, we can be sure that the *hokku* responded to the demands of its genre—that is, to the expectations of its audience.

EACH OF THE VERSES translated in this anthology was produced by a poet of experience and skill, each forms a complete statement, and each includes a season word that was taken from a list that was much shorter than the ones used by *haiku* poets of later times but was still a recognized list. In my choice of poets, I have aimed at breadth, including all the major *renga* masters of the late medieval and early modern periods but also a few poets who are overlooked in conventional histories. In my choice of poems, I have also stressed variety, to the extent possible given the sources involved. However, I have included only a few verses from *renga* masters that are more than slightly unorthodox, not because such verses, which fall under the rubric *haikai* (variously translated as "comic," "vulgar," or simply "unorthodox"), are unimportant or uninteresting, but because in many ways they deserve separate treatment. For those interested in these more immediate predecessors and contemporaries of Bashō, there are numerous sources already available in English. This book stresses the continuities and connections between Bashō and his forebears, even going so far as to include only *hokku* by Bashō that were actually composed for linked-verse sequences and opting for "original" versions rather than later revisions, whenever the latter are known.

In my past translations of *hokku*, I have generally attempted to render verses according to the traditional syllable count of 5-7-5 in order to reinforce a sense of the genetic relationship between *hokku* and earlier *uta*. In the spirit of a project attempting to emphasize the relationship between *hokku* and later *haiku*, I have chosen in this book to use a more condensed format, whenever possible.

Rather than encumber the text with notes, I have incorporated immediate contextual information, when available, into the headnotes of the poems, many of which contain information from a number of sources. I have also provided a short commentary for each poem, including the original Japanese text in romanized form, any allusions I have been able to identify, information of a historical nature, and, occasionally, a sentence or two of interpretation. My goal in presenting this material is to introduce readers to the contexts of the poems without overwhelming them with background detail.

Notes

For a list of the abbreviations used in the notes, see the bibliography.

1. Fujiwara no Kiyosuke, *Fukuro zōshi*, in SNKBT, vol. 29, p. 24.
2. Ibid.
3. Emperor Juntoku, *Yakumo mishō*, in NKT, supplementary vol. 3, pp. 203–206.
4. Fujiwara no Tameie, *Nishiki ka to aki wa sagano no miyuru kana*. The *renga* gathering is recorded in *Seiashō*, one of Tonna's critical treatises. See Steven D. Carter, *Just Living: Poems and Prose by the Japanese Monk Tonna* (New York: Columbia University Press, 2003), p. 205.
5. Carter, *Just Living*, p. 205.

6. Fujiwara no Tameuji, *Kikanu ni zo kokoro wa tsukusu hototogisu* (*Tsukubashū* 2082).
7. The comment is recorded in *Kensai zōdan*. See Steven D. Carter, "Chats with the Master: Selections from *Kensai Zōdan*," *Monumenta Nipponica* 56, no. 3 (2001): 312.
8. Quoted in Imawaga Ryōshun, *Rakusho roken*, in *Karon kagaku shūsei*, edited by Sasaki Takahiro et al. (Tokyo: Miyai shoten, 2001), vol. 10, p. 100.
9. Yoshida no Kenkō, "Essays in Idleness," translated by Steven D. Carter, in *Classical Japanese Prose: An Anthology*, compiled and edited by Helen Craig McCullough (Stanford, Calif.: Stanford University Press, 1990), p. 411.
10. Ryōshun, *Rakusho roken*, p. 100.
11. Ibid.
12. Nijō Yoshimoto, *Niwa ni mite tsuki no naka naru noyama kana* (*Tsukubashū* 2115).
13. Gusai, *Kumo kaeri kaze shizumarinu aki no ame* (*Tsukubashū* 2116).
14. Nijō Yoshimoto, *Renri hishō*, in NKBT, vol. 66, pp. 52–53.
15. Nijō Yoshimoto, *Tsukuba mondō*, in NKBT, vol. 66, p. 89.
16. Reizei Tamesuke, *Shimo kiete hikage ni nururu ochiba kana* (Nijō Yoshimoto, *Tsukuba mondō*, p. 89).
17. H. Mack Horton, "*Renga* Unbound: Performative Aspects of Linked Verse," *Harvard Journal of Asiatic Studies* 53 (1993): 443–512.
18. The text is known by the prolix title *Kitanosha ichimaku go-hokku, waki, daisan, narabi ni jo*. For further information, see Steven D. Carter, *Regent Redux: A Life of the Statesman-Scholar Ichijō Kaneyoshi* (Ann Arbor: Center for Japanese Studies, University of Michigan, 1996), pp. 44–48.
19. Matsuo Bashō, *Oi no kobumi*, in NKBZ, vol. 41, p. 311.
20. Such requests typically came immediately before the gathering, so the author of the *hokku* could include accurate seasonal imagery.
21. Matsuo Bashō, *Samidare o atsumete hayashi mogamigawa* (*Oku no hosomichi*, in NKBZ, vol. 41, p. 369).
22. Steven D. Carter, "On a Bare Branch: Bashō and the *Haikai* Profession," *Journal of the American Oriental Society* 117, no. 1 (1997): 57–69.
23. Matsuo Bashō, *Samidare o atsumete suzushi mogamigawa*. See the commentary to poem 281, in NKBZ, vol. 41, p. 170.
24. Ibid.
25. Tani Sōboku, *Tōfū renga hiji*, in NKBZ, vol. 51, p. 177.
26. Sōgi, *Azuma mondō*, in NKBT, vol. 66, p. 218.
27. Bashō was particularly harsh in his appraisal of Matsunaga Teitoku (1571–1653), whose influence was still strong in the late seventeenth century. See *Kyoraishō*, in NKBZ, vol. 51, p. 495.

28. Carter, *Just Living*, pp. 14–19.

29. Sōgi, *Akeba mata itsu ka wa koyoi aki no tsuki* (*Jinensai hokku* 1091).

30. Fujiwara no Teika, *Akeba mata aki no nakaba mo suginu beshi katabuku tsuki no oshiki nomi ka wa* (*SCSS* 261).

31. Quoted in Robert H. Brower, "Fujiwara Teika's *Maigetsushō*," *Monumenta Nipponica* 40, no. 4 (1985): 422. As Brower notes, there is some doubt about whether this part of the text in question is actually from Teika's hand, but there is no doubt that it was accepted as authentic by Sōgi and other poets of his day.

32. Inawashiro Kensai, *Kaze wa nashi hikari ya harau tsuki no kumo* (*Sono no chiri*, p. 843).

The Poems

The Nun Abutsu

1   *Composed on her way to the East Country, on the last day of the Ninth Month, when people planning a linked-verse party asked her for a* hokku

Here we are,
already—on the day
autumn ends.

2   *Composed when the same people asked for another* hokku *the next day*

Here we are,
again—on the day
winter begins.

Mushō

3   *Composed upon the request of Fujiwara no Tameuji at the temple of Ryūshin Shōnin in Fukakusa*

Cry out, then, cry—
crickets in the heavy dew
of Fukakusa.

Died 1283. Court lady and founder of the Reizei lineage.

AUTUMN   *Kyō wa haya aki no kagiri ni narinikeri* (Sōgi, *Azuma mondō,*
p. 218) ~East Country: here, the shogunal stronghold of Kamakura.
~Noble literati were often asked to provide first verses for sequences.
~One source attributes this verse (and the next one) to Abutsu's hus-
band, Fujiwara no Tameie (1198–1275). ~According to the lunar calendar,
autumn ended on the last day of the Ninth Month.

WINTER   *Kyō wa mata fuyu no hajime ni narinikeri* (Sōgi, *Azuma mondō,*
p. 218) ~According to the lunar calendar, winter began on the first day of
the Tenth Month.

Buddhist monk and early *renga* master.

AUTUMN   (dew) *Nake ya nake tsuyu fukakusa no kirigirisu* (Tonna,
Seiashō, p. 112) ~Fujiwara no Tameuji (1222–1286): head of the Miko-
hidari lineage of court poets. ~Ryūshin Shōnin: Enkū Ryūshin (1213–
1284), a Buddhist priest of the Pure Land sect associated with Shinshū'in
in Fukakusa. ~Fukakusa: a village in the Fushimi area, south of Kyoto.
~Compare *GSIS* 273, by Sone no Yoshitada (fl. ca. 980–1000): Cry out,
then, cry— / crickets in your tangle / of mugwort timber! / The passing
of autumn / is indeed so sad a time.

Zenna

4 *Composed beneath the cherry blossoms at Takao, when two 1000-verse
   events were held in one day*

Just a few blossoms—
a garland for the branches
of an old tree.

5 Dewdrops?
   Or moonlight forming
   in the grasses?

Reizei Tamesuke

6 Hazy or not,
   come out of the clouds,
   spring moon!

7 Frost melts—
   drenching fallen leaves
   in sunlight.

Buddhist monk of the Time sect and early *renga* master.

SPRING   (cherry blossoms) *Eda nokoru hana wa oiki no kazashi kana* (*Tsukubashū* 2044) ~Takao: a mountainous area northwest of Kyoto famous for the beauty of its foliage. ~The "old tree" stands for the poet, who represented older conventions of linked verse that were yielding to the new ways of Nijō Yoshimoto (p. 28).

AUTUMN   (dew, moon) *Tsuyu wa isa tsuki koso kusa ni musubikere* (*Tsukubashū* 2120).

1263–1328.   Son of Nun Abutsu (p. 20) and Fujiwara no Tameie, court poet, and longtime resident of Kamakura, where he served as *uta* master and literary jack-of-all-trades.

SPRING   (haze, spring moon) *Kasumu to mo kumo o ba ideyo haru no tsuki* (*Tsukubashū* 2039) ~Haze, usually a welcome sign of spring, here impedes the view.

WINTER   (frost) *Shimo kiete hikage ni nururu ochiba kana* (Nijō Yoshimoto, *Tsukuba mondō*, p. 89) ~The word "drenching" refers (literally) to frost melting onto fallen leaves and (figuratively) to sunlight that makes the leaves sparkle.

Musō Soseki

8   Come, sing now—
don't wait for *us* to wait,
cuckoo!

9   In waters
that know no summer
autumn bobs along.

Junkaku

10   *Composed on the first day of the Seventh Month*

Beneath a tree,
autumn wind shows itself
in a single leaf.

11   *For a 100-verse sequence composed at the home of Middle Counselor*
Taira no Munetsune

On leaves fallen
but not yet turned—
autumn showers.

1275–1351. Buddhist priest of the Rinzai Zen sect and major cultural figure, in politics as well as in poetry, garden design, and Zen discourse.

SUMMER   (cuckoo) *Kitsutsu nake matsu o na machi so hototogisu* (*Tsukubashū* 2085) ~The cuckoo's call was one of the harbingers of summer.

AUTUMN   *Natsu shiranu mizu koso aki o ukabekere* (*Tsukubashū* 2098) ~Water remains cool even in summer, promising autumn relief from the heat.

Disciple of Zenna (p. 22) and *renga* master.

AUTUMN   (autumn wind) *Kogakure ni akikaze misuru hitoha kana* (*Tsukubashū* 2103) ~The poem echoes a Chinese quotation from an early Han philosophical text, *Huainanzi* (*Master of Huainan*, 139 B.C.E.)—"See a single leaf fall, and you know the year is heading for its end"—that was well known in Japan as a proverb, often reduced to the phrase *kiri hitoha* (a single paulownia leaf). ~According to the lunar calendar, autumn began on the first day of the Seventh Month. As if recognizing that fact, a passing wind shows itself in a single trembling leaf.

AUTUMN   (fallen leaves, autumn showers) *Someakade ochiba ni kakaru shigure kana* (*Tsukubashū* 2135) ~Taira no Munetsune (1294–1349): a courtier associated with the Northern Court. ~Poetic convention had it that rain showers dyed autumn leaves, usually while still on the trees.

Gusai

12   *For a 100-verse sequence composed at the monument to Musō Soseki at Tenryūji*

Remember, now—
you are known for *singing*,
cuckoo!

13   *For a 100-verse sequence at the shrine at Anrakuji*

Not forgetting
the crimson of spring—
plum leaves.

14   *Composed at Kayadō, Mount Kōya*

On a thatched roof
it makes no sound at all—
autumn rain.

15   *Composed on the night of a full moon*

On such a night
only rain would not admire
the moon.

Died 1376. Buddhist monk and *renga* master, tutor of Nijō Yoshimoto (p. 28), and co-compiler of the first imperial anthology of linked verse, *Tsukubashū* (*Tsukuba Collection*, 1356).

SUMMER (cuckoo) *Nakeba koso na wa nokorikere hototogisu* (*Tsukubashū* 2086) ~Musō Soseki (p. 24). ~Tenryūji: a major Zen temple in Saga, west of Kyoto. ~An indirect way to encourage the cuckoo to do what it is known for—to sing!

AUTUMN (crimson plum leaves) *Kurenai o wasurenu ume no momiji kana* (*Tsukubashū* 2124) ~Anrakuji: a temple in Dazaifu, northern Kyūshū, dedicated to Sugawara no Michizane (845–903), who ended his days in exile there. ~Autumn is known for the red of maple leaves, but the leaves of the plum tree—known more for its spring blossoms—also turn red each autumn, showing the kind of constancy associated with the ever-loyal Michizane.

AUTUMN (autumn rain) *Oto kikanu kayaya no aki no shigure kana* (Takayama Sōzei, *Shoshin kyūeishū*, p. 64) ~Kayadō (literally, "thatched hall"): on Mount Kōya, in the mountainous region of Yoshino.

AUTUMN (moon) *Ame hitori tsuki o omowanu koyoi kana* (Takayama Sōzei, *Shoshin kyūeishū*, p. 64) ~Falling rain, here personified, would seek to conceal the moon and its beauty.

16   *Composed at Kiyomizu Temple in the Eleventh Month of 1341*

See snow as blossoms,
and underneath—
no bare limbs.

Nijō Yoshimoto

17   *Composed for a 100-verse sequence at Ishiyama on the eighteenth day of the Tenth Month of 1385*

Moon on the peak,
wind blowing into rain
on the Sea of Grebes.

18   *Composed when looking at autumn leaves at his mountain villa in the autumn of 1348*

The sun goes down—
but evening light remains
in the leaves.

19   *Composed on a visit to Gusai's cottage at Ōharano*

Which way to turn?
Winds in the autumn leaves,
snow in the pines.

WINTER   (snow) *Hana to mite yuki ni karetaru eda mo nashi* (*Tsukubashū* 2146) ~Kiyomizu Temple: a temple complex high on a slope off Fifth Avenue, in the Eastern Hills of Kyoto. ~A play on an old "confusion of the senses" here has philosophical effects.

1320–1388.   Heir of the noble Nijō branch of the Fujiwara family, imperial regent three times and major cultural figure, student of Gusai (p. 26), and co-compiler of *Tsukubashū*.

AUTUMN   (moon, rain) *Tsuki wa yama kaze zo shigure ni niho no umi* (*Ishiyama hyakuin*, p. 565) ~Ishiyamadera: a temple near the southern tip of the Sea of Grebes, or Lake Biwa. The *hyakuin* there involved Yoshimoto, Asayama Bontō (p. 32), Ninagawa Nobunaga, and others.

AUTUMN   (red leaves) *Hi wa irite momiji ni nokoru yūbe kana* (*Tsukubashū* 2126) ~So bright are the autumn leaves that for a moment one does not realize that the sun has gone down.

AUTUMN   (autumn leaves) *Izure min arashi no momiji matsu no yuki* (Takayama Sōzei, *Shoshin kyūeishū*, p. 63) ~A compliment to Gusai (p. 26) on the natural beauty on display around his cottage.

Shūa

20 *Composed on his first visit to the residence of the regent*

Storm winds
blow through blossoms—
becoming snow.

21 *Composed for a 1000-verse event at Kitano Shrine*

Gone down, I thought—
'til the moon emerged again
between clouds.

22 *Composed on a snowy day in the Tenth Month*

Coloring first
beneath light snow—
autumn leaves.

Sōa

23 Snow on pines,
green leaves on cherry limbs
—after storm winds.

24 Showers pass,
leaving the pines wet
but doing no more.

Buddhist monk, disciple of Gusai (p. 26), and one of the major poets of *Tsukubashū*.

SPRING (blossoms) *Hana ni fuki yuki ni nariyuku arashi kana* (Takayama Sōzei, *Mitsudenshō*, p. 117) ~Regent: Nijō Yoshimoto (p. 28).

AUTUMN (moon) *Iru to mite mata tsuki izuru kumoma kana* (*Tsukubashū* 2118) ~Kitano Shrine: a Shintō shrine on the northwestern edge of Kyoto. Inside its precincts was the *Renga* Bureau, where events sponsored by the shogunal government were held.

WINTER (snow) *Usuyuki o shita yori somuru momiji kana* (Takayama Sōzei, *Shoshin kyūeishū*, p. 65) ~Usually it is showers that dye the leaves, but here the first color comes from beneath a dusting of snow.

Renga master and priest at Konrenji, a temple of the Time sect on Fourth Avenue in Kyoto.

SPRING (cherry trees) *Matsu wa yuki hana wa aoba no arashi kana* (Shinkei, *Tokodokoro hentō*, p. 263) ~The wind arranges an exchange of foliage.

AUTUMN (showers) *Matsu no ha wa nururu bakari no shigure kana* (Shinkei, *Tokorodokoro hentō*, p. 263) ~Showers usually leave behind colored leaves, drawing attention away from the pines.

Asayama Bontō

25   I gaze at the moon—
      and every night is *the* night
      I had waited for.

26   *Composed at the residence of Lord Koga*

      Cold to the advances
      of rain in dawn moonlight—
      autumn leaves.

27   Mountains far-off
      in last night's moonlight—
      closer in morning snow.

28   Here by Fuji—
      never a moonlit night
      without snow.

1349–1427? Asayama Morotsuna: curator for the shogun Ashikaga Yoshimitsu (1358–1408), *uta* poet and *renga* master, and student of Nijō Yoshimoto (p. 28).

AUTUMN   (moon) *Miru tabi ni matareshi tsuki no koyoi kana* (Takayama Sōzei, *Shoshin kyūeishū*, p. 66) ~ The night is that night—the fifteenth day of the month—when the moon is full.

AUTUMN   (autumn leaves) *Ariake no ame ni tsurenaki konoha kana* (Takayama Sōzei, *Shoshin kyūeishū*, p. 66) ~Lord Koga: most likely Koga Tomomichi (1342–1397), a courtier. ~The word *tsurenashi* (cold, distant, to resist), a staple in love poems, here refers to the attitude of leaves toward rain.

WINTER   (snow) *Tsuki no yo no tōyama chikashi kesa no yuki* (Takayama Sōzei, *Shoshin kyūeishū*, p. 68).

WINTER   (snow) *Fuji nite wa yuki no yo naranu tsuki mo nashi* (Takayama Sōzei, *Kokon rendanshū*, p. 97) ~Elsewhere, the sight of snow and moonlight may be noteworthy, but on the peak of Fuji there is snow year-round.

Mitsuhiro

29 Patches of green—
paler here, brighter there
on snowy fields.

30 On a light breeze,
the heavy scent of blossoms
at morning.

31 Blow, winds!—
in those reeds sparkling
in evening moonlight.

32 Seared by frost
through the Long Month—
leaves on the trees.

Fushiminomiya Sadafusa

33 *Composed at Daikōmyōji on the third day of the Third Month of 1424*

Blossoms—of snow.
Branches, too, aging
on an old tree.

Died 1439–1441?   Samurai of the Mashimo clan in service to the shogun Ashikaga Yoshinori (1394–1441), later a lay monk known as Kei'a, and student of Asayama Bontō (p. 32).

SPRING   (green, lingering snow) *Usuku koki midori no nobe no yukima kana* (Shinkei, *Tokorodokoro hentō*, p. 262) ~Early in the New Year, spring shows itself in patches of green on fields still covered with snow.

SPRING   (blossoms) *Kaze yuruku hana kōbashiki ashita kana* (Shinkei, *Tokorodokoro hentō*, p. 263).

AUTUMN   (reeds) *Fuke arashi ogi ni honomeku yūzukuyo* (Shinkei, *Tokorodokoro hentō*, p. 263) ~The beauty of the moonlight in swaying reeds makes the bite in the autumn wind bearable.

WINTER   (frost) *Nagatsuki no shimo ni utsurou konoha kana* (Shinkei, *Tokorodokoro hentō*, p. 263) ~The Ninth Month of the lunar calendar was also known as the Long Month.

1372–1456.   Imperial prince whose son and heir became emperor (Go-Hanazono, 1419–1471, r. 1428–1464) and longtime resident of Fushimi, south of Kyoto, where he sponsored a literary salon.

SPRING   (blossoms) *Hana mo yuki eda mo furitaru oiki kana* (Fushiminomiya Sadafusa, *Kanmon nikki*, p. 425) ~Daikōmyōji: a Zen temple in Fushimi, south of Kyoto, near Sadafusa's residence. His diary records that he, one of his cleric brothers, and some retainers and friends were viewing the blossoms there when this *hokku* was written.

34   *For a 100-verse sequence composed on the twenty-fifth day of the Second Month of 1424*

Tomorrow!—bloom *then*,
blossoms I await
on a rainy night.

35   *For a 100-verse sequence composed on the twenty-fifth day of the Fourth Month of 1437*

Deutzia in bloom:
even at midday, moonlight
beneath the trees.

36   *For a 100-verse sequence composed on the twenty-fifth day of the Seventh Month of 1425*

In the pines, rain.
In the wind, autumn—
evening.

Chiun

37   *On "Blossoms"*

Ah, the capital—
at least one cherry tree
at every house.

SPRING (blossoms) *Asu wa sake hana matsu koro no yoru no ame* (Fushiminomiya Sadafusa, *Kanmon nikki shihai monjo*, p. 173) ~Sadafusa's diary records snow on the night of the twenty-third and rain on the night of the twenty-fifth, revealing that the poet's worries were not just posturing. The twenty-fifth day of every month was the established day for a *tsukinamikai* (monthly meeting) for Sadafusa's circle at the time.

SUMMER (deutzia) *Unohana wa hiru mo tsuki moru ko no ma kana* (Fushiminomiya Sadafusa, *Kanmon nikki shihai monjo*, p. 370) ~The deutzia—named, in English, after a German sponsor of the botanist who "discovered" it in Japan—produces white flowers in early summer.

AUTUMN *Matsu wa ame kaze wa aki naru yūbe kana* (Fushiminomiya Sadafusa, *Kanmon nikki shihai monjo*, p. 157) ~Sadafusa's diary records rain on the twenty-fifth and flooding over the next few days.

Died 1448. Ninagawa Chikamasa (lay name): high-ranking samurai in service to the Ashikaga shogunate, later a lay monk; student of the *uta* poet Shōtetsu (1381–1459); and one of Sōgi's Seven Sages of Linked Verse.

SPRING (blossoms) *Hana hitoki uenu miyako no yado mo nashi* (*Shinsen Tsukubashū* 3658) ~Cherry trees in city yards were, of course, planted or transplanted trees and as such symbolized the elegant tastes of their owners.

38   These, too, so lush?
        Leaves on the cherry trees
        in summer groves.

39   *On "Flowers on the Grasses," composed near Nakagawa on the nine-*
        teenth day of the Eighth Month of 1447

        Nameless grasses—
        in flower all along
        a river bank.

40   *Composed for a monthly* renga *meeting at the Ōhashi house*

        Which flowers fade?
        Any near chrysanthemums
        in bloom.

41   *Composed in the Eastern Hills*

        Mountain winds
        make a leafy waterfall—
        but no pool.

42   *"Snow"*

        Moon and snow—
        one hue 'til parting comes
        at daybreak.

SUMMER   (summer groves) *Hana no e mo kaku naru mono ka natsu ko-dachi* (*Shinsen Tsukubashū* 3697) ~Sōgi praised this *hokku* for its straight-forward simplicity (*Azuma mondō*, p. 220).

AUTUMN   (flowering grasses) *Na mo shiranu kokusa hana saku kawabe kana* (*Shinsen Tsukubashū* 3745) ~Nakagawa: a stream running along Eastern Kyōgoku Avenue in Kyoto. ~Compare a rustic scene in the "Lavender" chapter of *Genji monogatari* (*The Tale of Genji*, early eleventh century) on the morning after Genji has had his first conversation with Murasaki's uncle, the bishop, about his sister and her little girl: "There were heavy mists in the dawn sky, and bird songs came from Genji knew not where. Flowering trees and grasses *which he could not identify* spread like a tapestry before him" (Murasaki Shikibu, *Tale of Genji*, p. 93 [italics added]).

AUTUMN   (chrysanthemums) *Utsurou wa kiku saku koro no kusaki kana* (*Shinsen Tsukubashū* 3774) ~Ōhashi house: unidentified. ~By the time chrysanthemums flower in the autumn, most other flowers have faded; those that have not are put to shame by the chrysanthemums' vibrant colors.

WINTER   (falling leaves) *Yamakaze ni yodo naki taki no ochiba kana* (*Chikurinshō* 1791) ~Eastern Hills: Higashiyama, the mountains along the eastern border of the Kyoto basin. ~Leaves cascade down on mountain winds, but do not accumulate in a pool below.

WINTER   (snow) *Tsuki yuki no iro wakareyuku ashita kana* (*Shinsen Tsukubashū* 3837) ~In the dark of night, the moon and the snow appear to be the same color; in the light of dawn, however, the colors "part company."

43　*Composed at the house of Mochimasu, Master of the Left Capital*

A cold year—
not a single day
without snowfall.

Takayama Sōzei

44　*Composed on "Willows," for a gathering held to see someone off to the East Country*

In spring
they beckon passersby—
willow boughs.

45　Bitter sundown—
when even dusk fades
from the blossoms.

46　Kimono sleeves
brimming with happiness—
spring haze.

WINTER   (snow) *Toshi samushi hitohi mo furanu yuki wa nashi* (Chiun, *Chikamasa kushū* 61) ~Mochimasu: Toki Mochimasu (1406–1474), shogunal deputy of Mino Province. ~The last days of the year always seem dreary, even more so when snow falls day after day.

Died 1455. High-ranking samurai who served as *renga* steward (*sōshō*)—a laureate of sorts who was in charge of the *Renga* Bureau of Kitano Shrine—of the Ashikaga shogunate, student of the *uta* poet Shōtetsu (1381–1459), and one of Sōgi's Seven Sages of Linked Verse.

SPRING   (willows) *Harukaze ni yuku hito shitau yanagi kana* (*Shinsen Tsukubashū* 3624) ~Sōzei's personal anthology identifies the traveler as the Lord of Koga, perhaps referring to Ashikaga Shigeuji (1434–1497), who set off as shogunal deputy to the Kantō (Kantō Kubō) in 1449. ~In China, willows were given as parting gifts. Here, the willow branches blow from the east, as though welcoming the traveler.

SPRING   (blossoms) *Hi zo oshiki hana wa yūbe no iro mo nashi* (*Shinsen Tsukubashū* 3652) ~After sunset, the blossoms will lack even the muted hues of dusk.

SPRING   (haze) *Ureshisa o tsutsumu tamoto ka harugasumi* (Takayama Sōzei, *Zeikahokku* 1428) ~Since all the *hokku* in this collection are on flowers, the reader is doubtless meant to read the "happiness" as flowers adorning the spring haze.

47 *For a 100-verse sequence composed on the sixth day of the Fifth Month*

Wilted by morning:
eaves of sweet flag—a woman
on a one-night stand.

48 *Composed in the Sixth Month*

How cool it is!
In summer, beneath trees
as if in flower.

49 A grove
of brushes dipped in red?
Autumn trees.

50 *Composed in the Tenth Month*

Answering the sound
of rain as they too fall—
autumn leaves.

51 *Composed in the Twelfth Month*

Storm winds
sweep snow from pines—
a jeweled broom.

SUMMER   (irises) *Kesa karuru ayame ya noki no hitoyotsuma* (*Shinsen Tsukubashū* 3712) ~Compare *SIS* 109, by Ōnakatomi no Yoshitane: 'Til yesterday / I had no regard at all / for sweet flag. / Now it has quite taken over / as the Lady of the House! ~For the Sweet Flag Festival—on the fifth day of the Fifth Month—people stuffed their eaves with sweet flag in hopes of warding off illness. The poem involves plays on words (*karuru* meaning both "wither" and "depart," and *tsuma* meaning both "wife" and the "edge" of the eaves), which my translation fails to convey.

SUMMER   (cool) *Suzushisa o natsu wa hana naru kokage kana* (*Chikurinshō* 1703) ~The cool beneath the trees brings back memories of spring blossoms.

AUTUMN   (autumn trees) *Kurenai no fude no hayashi ka kigi no aki* (Takayama Sōzei, *Sōzei hokku narabi ni tsukeku nukigaki* 1882) ~An example of the kind of extravagant metaphor for which Sōzei was well known.

AUTUMN   (autumn leaves) *Chiru oto o shigure ni kaesu momiji kana* (Takayama Sōzei, *Sōzei ku* 1068) ~As if in reply to the tapping of the rain in the trees, leaves too make a sound when they strike the ground.

WINTER   (snow) *Yuki harau arashi ya matsu no tamahahaki* (Takayama Sōzei, *Sōzei ku* 1074) ~Wind blows snowflakes from pine limbs, creating the impression of a broom of jewels.

Gyōjo

52   Who would guess
they could ever scatter?
Cherries in full bloom.

53   *On "Escaping the Heat"*

Hearts are one
in the cool shade
of a single pine.

54   *Composed on the first day of autumn*

Dew-laden,
it falls without wind—
a single leaf.

55   The sound
of brocade in the making?
Rain in glowing leaves.

56   Giving color
to rain, sound to snow—
showers of sleet.

57   *Composed on the twenty-fifth day of the Twelfth Month of 1454, on the
idea of "Year's End"*

Ah, for a year
that did not fade with light
from white snow.

1405–1469. Samurai in service to the Yamana clan, later a lay monk; student of Takayama Sōzei (p. 40); and one of Sōgi's Seven Sages of Linked Verse.

SPRING   (cherry blossoms) *Chiru beku mo oboenu hana no sakari kana* (Gyōjo, *Gyōjo kushū* 1410).

SUMMER   (cool) *Kage suzushi tare mo kokoro ya hitotsumatsu* (*Chikurinshō* 1702) ~Summer heat is something so elemental that it makes us all the same.

AUTUMN   (dew) *Tsuyu nagara chiru wa kaze naki hitoha kana* (*Shinsen Tsukubashū* 3731) ~The advent of autumn is usually heralded by wind, but here it is by the fall of a leaf burdened with dew.

AUTUMN   (glowing leaves) *Nishiki oru oto ka momiji no hatsushigure* (*Chikurinshō* 1770) ~The rich and varied colors of autumn leaves are often compared to the look of brocade, but here the focus is on sound—the patter of rain on the leaves, calling to mind the rattle of a loom.

WINTER   (sleet) *Ame ni iro yuki ni koe aru mizore kana* (*Chikurinshō* 1804) ~Sleet is somewhere between rain and snow, boasting sensory features that enhance the experience of both.

WINTER   (snow) *Shirayuki no hikari ni kurenu toshi mogana* (*Shinsen Tsukubashū* 3850) ~White snow signals that winter is not ready to concede, despite the approach of the New Year.

Nōa

58   Spend yourself *now*!
Spring winds blowing
before cherries bloom.

59   *On "Wildflowers," composed for a gathering at the* Renga Bureau of
Kitano Shrine

River winds
spread wildflower scent
across the fields.

60   *From among his autumn* hokku

Autumn winds
show leaves' undersides—
gusts of white.

61   Autumn disrobes—
casting off a brocade
of falling leaves.

1397–1471. Buddhist monk, painter, *renga* master and *renga* steward at Kitano Shrine, curator for the Ashikaga shogunate, and one of Sōgi's Seven Sages of Linked Verse.

SPRING (spring winds, cherry blossoms) *Fukitsukuse hana sakanu ma no haru no kaze* (*Chikurinshō* 1591) ~Compare *SIS* 1035, anonymous: Spring wind— / spend yourself *now*, / before the cherries bloom. / Then I can gaze without worry / when their season comes.

AUTUMN (wildflowers) *Kawakaze no fukiageniou hanano kana* (*Chikurinshō* 1720) ~Kitano Shrine: formally Kitano Tenmangū, in northwestern Kyoto. Tenjin shrines were dedicated to Sugawara no Michizane (845–903), to one of whose poems Nōa alludes: White chrysanthemums / blown by rising winds / at Fukiage Strand. / But are they truly flowers? / Or perhaps approaching waves? (*KKS* 272) ~The *hokku* may come from the time when Nōa was *renga* steward at the shrine.

AUTUMN (autumn winds) *Uraba fuku akikaze shiroki kozue kana* (*Shinsen Tsukubashū* 3771) ~Chinese cosmology associated autumn with coolness and with the color white (as spring with green, summer with orange, and winter with deep, dark red), here expressed by wind showing the pale undersides of leaves.

WINTER (falling leaves) *Aki no nugu nishiki wa kigi no ochiba kana* (*Chikurinshō* 1773) ~The poem evokes the image of the Maiden of Tatsuta, a mythological creature associated with weaving, dyeing, and autumn leaves. Mount Tatsuta, near Nara, was famous for its autumn colors.

Shinkei

62   A misty bridge
and at riverside, the green—
of willows.

63   *Composed when he was viewing the blossoms at Daigo Jakuseidani*

Ah, the deep woods—
so quiet one can hear
blossoms fall.

64   *From among his spring* hokku

Not seen at blossom time:
dusk deepening
in green leaves.

65   Spring wanes,
warblers leave—
blossoms gone, too.

66   Hide yourself, cuckoo,
from those who did not wait
for your call.

67   Haze over all—
and a mountain path rife
with bellsounds.

1406–1475. Bishop of the Jūjūshin'in (a Tendai temple in Kyoto), student of the *uta* poet Shōtetsu (1381–1459), author of numerous critical works, and one of Sōgi's Seven Sages of Linked Verse.

SPRING   (willows) *Hashi kasumu kawabe ni aoki yanagi kana* (Shinkei, *Shibakusa kunai hokku* 493).

SPRING   (blossoms) *Chiru hana no oto kiku hodo no miyama kana* (*Chikurinshō* 1639) ~Daigoji: a Shingon temple in Fushimi, south of Kyoto. Jakuseidani (Valley of Calm and Quiet) was in a secluded area behind the temple.

SPRING   (green leaves) *Hana ni minu yūgure fukaki aoba kana* (*Shinsen Tsukubashū* 3677) ~Precisely because of their beauty, blossoms can be a distraction. For the discerning, the green growth of spring at dusk also has its allure.

SPRING   (warblers, blossoms) *Haru oite uguisu kaeri hana mo nashi* (Shinkei, *Shibakusa kunai hokku* 117) ~An example of the understated, austere style for which Shinkei is famous.

SUMMER   (cuckoo) *Matade kiku hito ni wa shinobe hototogisu* (Shinkei, *Shibakusa kunai hokku* 170) ~A common theme in classical poetry: only the properly attentive should share aesthetic delights.

SUMMER   (rife) *Kasumikeri yamaji ya shigeru kane no koe* (Shinkei, *Shibakusa kunai hokku* 192) ~A superb example of how even a short *hokku* can end unexpectedly—not with the "green growth" that one would anticipate, but with the sound of temple bells.

68   Not producing
      even a mountain echo—
      cicadas' drone.

69   *Composed on the night of the fifteenth day of the Eighth Month*

      Moon gazing,
      I forget that tonight
      is *the* night.

70   *Composed when viewing the moon after spending many years in the*
      East Country

      In moonlight
      I remember—then forget—
      the capital.

71   Next storm,
      not a leaf will scatter
      on the wind.

72   Curse the luck!
      Rushing gets you wetter
      in a passing shower.

73   Frozen, it seems—
      Mount Fuji floating
      in the autumn sea.

74   From bare brush
      along a mountain path—
      the sound of frost.

SUMMER (cicadas) *Yamabiko mo kotae ya aenu semi no koe* (Shinkei, *Shibakusa kunai hokku* 236) ~The drone of the cicadas in the trees is so unrelenting that there is no time for an echo to form. Or maybe so weak?

AUTUMN (moon) *Nagametsutsu tsuki ni wasururu koyoi kana* (*Chikurinshō* 1739) ~So captivating is the moon that one forgets that the fifteenth is the night of the full moon.

AUTUMN (moon) *Tsuki ni koi tsuki ni wasururu miyako kana* (*Shinsen Tsukubashū* 3768) ~Shinkei fled the capital at the beginning of the Ōnin War (1467–1477) and ended up spending his last years in the East Country. The sight of the moon—a reminder of his home in Kyoto, where moon gazing was a common activity—brings both heartache and consolation.

AUTUMN (scattering leaves) *Mata fukeba hitoha wa chiranu arashi kana* (Shinkei, *Shibakusa kunai hokku* 247) ~An oblique way of describing the power of a storm raging now.

AUTUMN (shower) *Ayaniku ni isogeba nururu shigure kana* (Shinkei, *Shibakusa kunai hokku* 352) ~There are gaps in autumn showers, but they are too unpredictable to chase after.

AUTUMN (autumn sea) *Kōru rashi fuji o ukaburu aki no umi* (Shinkei, *Shibakusa kunai hokku* 444) ~In the East Country, Shinkei had frequent occasion to see Fuji, which was not far down the coast southwest of his home.

AUTUMN (bare brush, frost) *Kareshiba ni shimo no koe kiku yamaji kana* (Shinkei, *Shibakusa kunai hokku* 362) ~An example of the aesthetic ideal that Shinkei called *hiesabi* (chill and sere).

75 A lull in the wind—
    and autumn leaves descend
    closer to the trees.

76 Is it so late?
    How cold the river sounds
    in moonlit dusk.

77 Near my eaves
    birds chirp in the snow
    at morning.

78 After autumn gales,
    no snow is left to break
    the branches.

79 Showers fall—
    but mountain pines
    are untainted still.

80 Stars shining—white.
    Goose-cries freezing
    in midnight sky.

AUTUMN   (autumn leaves) *Kaze no ma wa kokage ni otsuru momiji kana* (Shinkei, *Shibakusa kunai hokku* 364) ~During pauses in the wind, the leaves pile up directly beneath the trees.

WINTER   (cold) *Fukenuru ka kawaoto samuki yūzukuyo* (Shinkei, *Shibakusa kunai hokku* 382) ~The bright sound of the river reveals the growing chill in the air at dusk.

WINTER   (snow) *Noki chikaku tori naku yuki no ashita kana* (Shinkei, *Shibakusa kunai hokku* 389) ~Inside his house, the speaker hears something unexpected on a snowy morning—a birdcall that reminds him of approaching spring but also makes him more aware of the cold.

WINTER   (snow) *Nowaki seshi kusaki wa oruru yuki mo nashi* (Shinkei, *Shibakusa kunai hokku* 417) ~A conception reminiscent of that in poem 71: autumn storms broke so many branches that there is no place left for the weight of snow to have its effect.

WINTER   (showers) *Shigurete mo matsu wa misao no yamabe kana* (Shinkei, *Shibakusa kunai hokku* 418) ~ "Untainted" translates *misao*, the same word that means "innocence" and "chastity." Other trees change color, but the pine is a constant green.

WINTER   (frozen) *Hoshi shiroshi kari ga ne kōru yowa no sora* (Shinkei, *Shibakusa kunai hokku* 486).

Senjun

81   Morning haze
hides blossoms from the wind—
too completely!

82   Cherries in full bloom—
think of them, and no clouds
can compare.

83   Dew on grasses,
withstanding the wind?
No—fireflies.

84   *Composed for a meeting held on the tenth day of the Seventh Month*

Crickets sing—
and my moon-waiting
begins at morning.

85   Brighter here,
paler there, the leaves—
after scattered showers.

1411–1476. Buddhist priest, student of the *uta* poet Shōtetsu (1381–1459), master of flower arrangement and *renga*, disciple of Takayama Sōzei (p. 40), and one of Sōgi's Seven Sages of Linked Verse.

SPRING   (haze) *Asagasumi kaze ni kakusu ya hana mo nashi* (*Chikurinshō* 1597) ~Seeking to conceal blossoms from the wind, the morning haze obscures the flowers altogether.

SPRING   (cherry blossoms) *Hanazakari omoeba nitaru kumo mo nashi* (*Shinsen Tsukubashū* 3640) ~The preface to *Kokinshū* (*Collection of Ancient and Modern Poems*, ca. 905) says the poet Kakinomoto no Hitomaro (ca. 660–710) compared cherry blossoms in Yoshino to clouds. Senjun says there is really no comparison. ~Compare *SCSS* 72, by Fujiwara no Ietaka (1158–1237): This morning, / I gaze out at clouds / engulfed by cherry blossoms— / and at haze that cannot conceal / the mountains of Yoshino.

SUMMER   (fireflies) *Kaze ni tsuyu kienu kusaba no hotaru kana* (*Chikurinshō* 1691) ~Compare *Shōji shodo hyakushu* 1200, by Lady Sanuki (ca. 1141–ca. 1217): Through the night, / fireflies cling to the leaves / on the grasses— / looking like dewdrops / undislodged by the wind.

AUTUMN   (crickets) *Higurashi no koe ni tsuki matsu ashita kana* (*Shinsen Tsukubashū* 3738) ~The very word *higurashi* (cricket) means "end of day," but here a cricket's song comes at morning.

AUTUMN   (colored leaves, showers) *Usuku koki momiji ya itsu no murashigure* (*Shinsen Tsukubashū* 3789) ~Scattered showers make for a chiaroscuro effect in the foliage.

86 Painted
    in pale black ink—
    snowy dusk.

87 Morning river—
    bound with a sash
    of ice.

88 "Look—snow!"
    —says the wind, rolling
    up the blinds.

89 *From among his winter* hokku

    Trees unbroken
    by the weight of snow—
    thanks to strong winds.

Sugiwara Sōi

90 *For a meeting at the home of an acquaintance who lived near Horikawa*

    Reflections
    of stars, on the riverbank?
    Plum blossoms.

91 The Fifth Month comes—
    and a light shower counts
    as a lull in the rain.

WINTER (snow) *Usuzumi ni egakeru yuki no yūbe kana* (*Shinsen Tsukubashū* 3842) ~Ink-wash painting, a genre borrowed from China, was a major development of Japan's medieval era.

WINTER (ice) *Asakawa wa obi o musuberu kōri kana* (Senjun, *Hōgen Senjun kushū* 268).

WINTER (snow) *Yuki miyo to sudare fukimaku arashi kana* (Senjun, *Hōgen Senjun kushū* 269) ~*Sudare* are horizontal hanging blinds, usually made of bamboo.

WINTER (snow) *Yuki orenu ki wa mina kaze no chikara kana* (*Chikurinshō* 1831) ~A conception reminiscent of that in poems 71 and 78: the power of the wind has removed the burden of the snow's weight.

1418–1485. Sugiwara Katamori: samurai in service to the Ashikaga shogunate, *renga* steward, and one of Sōgi's Seven Sages of Linked Verse.

SPRING (plum blossoms) *Kage utsuru hoshi ka kawabe no ume no hana* (*Chikurinshō* 1568) ~Horikawa: a stream running north–south along the eponymous Hori Street in Kyoto.

SUMMER (Fifth Month) *Samidare no ame komaka naru harema kana* (*Chikurinshō* 1685) ~So constant are the rains of early summer that a fine sprinkle constitutes a moment of respite.

92   So cold a rain
that the trees are dripping—
with icicles.

93   Plum trees blossom—
and my spring wait
is over.

Sōgi

94   *Composed in the East Country, for a gathering at the mountain cottage of Ōta, the lay monk governor of Bitchū*

Glimpses of white
between blinds of haze—
snow on the peaks.

95   Birds cry out—
at those who pick blossoms
on the mountain path.

96   *On "Falling Blossoms," from a 100-verse sequence composed at the home of Lord Sasaki, governor of Ōmi*

In a world
of lies—why not blossoms
that *don't* fall?

WINTER   (icicles) *Ame samumi shizuku o kigi no taruhi kana* (*Chikurinshō* 1801).

WINTER   (plum trees) *Ume sakite hana ni matsu beki haru mo nashi* (*Chikurinshō* 1835) ~The word "blossoms" usually refers to cherry blossoms, whose blooming is the most treasured moment of spring. Sōi instead praises the plum, which blooms much earlier in the season.

1421–1502.   Zen monk; disciple of Takayama Sōzei (p. 40) and Senjun (p. 54), also greatly influenced by Shinkei (p. 48); among the chief compilers of *Shinsen Tsukubashū* (*New Tsukuba Collection*, mid-1490s); and author of numerous critical works as well as travel journals and a collection of *uta* poetry.

SPRING   (haze) *Hima shiroki kasumi ya sudare mine no yuki* (Sōgi, *Jinensai hokku* 61) ~Ōta: Ōta Dōkan (1432–1486), a warlord and the governor of Bitchū Province. ~An echo, perhaps, of poem 88.

SPRING   (blossoms) *Oru hito ni tori naku hana no yamaji kana* (Sōgi, *Jinensai hokku* 214).

SPRING   (blossoms) *Itsuwari no aru yo ni chiranu hana mogana* (Sōgi, *Jinensai hokku* 369) ~Lord Sasaki: probably Rokkaku Sasaki Ujiyori (d. 1518), the governor of Ōmi Province. ~Buddhism teaches that the world is an illusion and all statements are in that sense lies. The poet asks, "If so, why can't we have any choice in how lies work? Why not blossoms that don't fall?"

97 *On "Summer Moon," composed at Insetsuji in Izumi Sakai*

The moon falls—
as morning tide ebbs swiftly
on the summer sea.

98 Sounding in the trees,
rising toward the sky—
a bubbling spring.

99 *Composed for a 1000-verse event at the Ise provincial offices, on the topic "Relief from the Heat"*

Ah, for blossoms—
to bring gusts of wind
to my summer garden.

100 *On "Relief from the Heat," composed at the house of Kanbō Hachirō*

Splashing cool
over a boulder—
pebbles of water.

101 Cooler still
after I leave it—
the shade of the trees.

102 The peak clears—
river mists white
in morning sun.

SUMMER   (summer sea) *Tsuki otsuru asashio hayashi natsu no umi*
(Sōgi, *Jinensai hokku* 733) ~Insetsuji: a temple of the Time sect. ~Izumi
Sakai: the modern-day Osaka area, which was a major commercial port
in the medieval period. ~Summer nights are short as it is, and when the
moon goes down the tide seems to rush away with it.

SUMMER   (spring) *Kigi ni hibiki kumo ni minagiru izumi kana* (Sōgi, *Ji-
nensai hokku* 805) ~The echo of the spring in the trees makes it seem as if
the water is vaulting up into the sky.

SUMMER   (summer garden) *Hana mogana arashi ya towamu natsu no
niwa* (Sōgi, *Jinensai hokku* 810) ~*Hokku* composed for 1000-verse se-
quences were often written on assigned topics (*dai*). ~Why hope for
blossoms, only for wind to assault them? In order to obtain relief from
summer heat.

SUMMER   (cool) *Iwao yori kudakete suzushi sazaremizu* (Sōgi, *Jinensai
hokku* 821) ~Kanbō Hachirō: a member of the Kanbō clan, otherwise un-
identified, deputy constables (*shugodai*) of a district in Etchū Province.

SUMMER   (cool) *Tachisarite suzushisa masaru kokage kana* (Sōgi, *Jinen-
sai hokku* 911) ~As Inawashiro Kensai (p. 84) says, it is only after going back
out into the heat that one truly appreciates a tree's shade (*Kensai zōdan*,
p. 414).

AUTUMN   (mists) *Mine harete kawakiri shiroki asahi kana* (Sōgi, *Jinen-
sai hokku* 1055) ~When the clouds lift and the morning sun shines down,
the mist—a murky gray just moments before—turns white.

103 *Composed on the night of a full moon at the house of Nagao, governor of Mikawa, when the world was in turmoil*

My days may be few—
yet I cannot complain
to such a moon.

104 *Composed when he was visiting Uji*

In murky dawn
the moon takes leave
of its light.

105 *Scribbled down when he happened to be in Naniwa*

In pine wind
bellsounds shower down
with evening rain.

106 Spring rains began
and in no time at all—
rotten leaves.

107 *For a meeting at Enkō'in, Honnōji*

Does water rise?
Frozen up in the sky,
the moon.

AUTUMN   (moon) *Nokoru mi o tsuki ni kakotanu koyoi kana* (Sōgi, *Ji-nensai hokku* 1093) ~Nagao, governor of Mikawa: Nagao Sukekage, a retainer of Uesugi Akisada (1454–1510). ~The "turmoil" probably refers to the Ōnin War (1467–1477), which raged on and off in the Kyoto basin. Sōgi spent much of his time in the East Country during the war years.

AUTUMN   (moon) *Asaborake tsuki ni wakaruru hikari kana* (Sōgi, *Jinen-sai hokku* 1127) ~Uji: an area just south of Kyoto, well known especially as a place to enjoy the moon shining on Lake Ogura and the River Uji. ~As night gives way to dawn, the moon must fade, "parting" from its light.

AUTUMN   (showers) *Matsukaze ni kane mo shigururu yūbe kana* (Sōgi, *Jinensai hokku* 1340) ~Compare poem 67.

WINTER   (rotten leaves) *Harusame no someshi ma mo naki kuchiba kana* (Sōgi, *Jinensai hokku* 1405) ~Spring showers began the process of change that ends now in rotting leaves, devoid of color.

WINTER   (frozen) *Noboru mizu arite ya kōru sora no tsuki* (Sōgi, *Jinensai hokku* 1449) ~Honnōji: a Hokke temple complex in central Kyoto. ~A fanciful conception reminiscent of Takayama Sōzei (p. 40).

108   *Composed for a meeting held by Nagao, governor of Shimōsa*

Damming water,
then forsaking it to ice—
rotting leaves.

109   *Composed at the house of Lord Ikeda of Wakasa*

Water, white—
what remains of sleet
in the garden.

110   *On "Hail"*

Who could it be—
up in the sky, breaking ice
into jewels of hail?

111   *On "Snow," composed at the house of Utsunomiya Matsatsuna*

The pond, clear
with cold mountain water—
reflecting snow.

112   No hint of wind—
but waiting in the bamboo
is morning snow.

WINTER   (ice, rotting leaves) *Seku mizu o kōri ni yuzuru kuchiba kana* (Sōgi, *Jinensai hokku* 1467) ~Nagao: a retainer of Uesugi Fusasada (d. 1494), the governor of Shimōsa Province, and a disciple of Sōgi. ~First, leaves "occupied" the water, later giving way to ice.

WINTER   (sleet) *Mizu shiroki niwa wa mizore no nagori kana* (Sōgi, *Jinensai hokku* 1488) ~Lord Ikeda of Wakasa: Fujiwara Masatane (often called Ikeda, after the region of Settsu Province [the northern part of modern-day Osaka Prefecture], where he lived), an important patron of poets and artists. ~What accounts for the white sheen of the puddles in the garden? Sleet not yet melted.

WINTER   (ice, hail) *Sora ni ta ga kudaku kōri zo tamaarare* (Sōgi, *Jinensai hokku* 1489).

WINTER   (snow) *Ike harete yamamizu samushi yuki no kage* (Sōgi, *Jinensai hokku* 1519) ~Utsunomiya Masatsuna: head of the Utsunomiya house, based in the city of that name in Shimotsuke Province (modern-day Tochigi Prefecture). ~Come summer, pond water will be stagnant and murky, but a fresh infusion of snowmelt from the mountains makes it clear enough to reflect snow on the peaks.

WINTER   (snow) *Kaze ya naki take ni machitoru kesa no yuki* (Sōgi, *Jinensai hokku* 1566) ~Poems about snow blown from branches by wind are commonplace.

113 *On "First Snow," composed at Kinrinji in Tamba Province*

First snow:
no dust in the garden,
none in my heart.

114 *For a memorial* renga *meeting held by Ogasawara Sōgen at the end of
the year during which Sugiwara Sōi had died*

The world I knew
darkens into dreams
at year's end.

Hino Tomiko

115 *Composed during the year after her son Ashikaga Yoshihisa had died*

Sadly, I live on—
in a world of deutzia
in full bloom.

116 Unsullied
by the pond water below—
lotuses.

WINTER   (first snow) *Hatsuyuki no niwa wa kokoro no chiri mo nashi* (Sōgi, *Jinensai hokku* 1573) ~Kinrinji: a Shūgendō temple in the modern-day Kameoka area, just west of Kyoto. ~A statement of gratitude to Sōgi's hosts at the temple. Rooms opening on garden space were favored as venues for poetry gatherings.

WINTER   (year's end) *Nareshi yo wa yume ni kureyuku kotoshi kana* (Sōgi, *Jinensai hokku* 1631) ~Ogasawara Sōgen: Ogasawara Noringa, the governor of Mino Province. Like Sugiwara Sōi (p. 56), who is said to have studied the military arts under Ogasawara tutelage, Sōgen was a samurai in service to the Ashikaga shogunate. ~Year's end is always a melancholy time, even more so when one is mourning the loss of a friend. Sōi was the last of Sōgi's Seven Sages of Linked Verse to pass away, on the twenty-eighth day of the Eleventh Month of 1485.

1440–1496.   Principal wife of the shogun Ashikaga Yoshimasa (1436–1490), major patron of the arts, and powerful political figure.

SUMMER   (deutzia) *Nagararu yo o unohana no sakari kana* (*Shinsen Tsukubashū* 3704) ~Ashikaga Yoshihisa (1465–1489): a son of Tomiko and the ninth shogun of the Ashikaga line. He died on the twenty-sixth day of the Third Month of 1489, at the age of twenty-five. Deutzia bloom in the Fourth Month, so her *hokku* may have been composed for a service marking the one-month anniversary of his death.

SUMMER   (lotuses) *Shitamizu ni nigoranu ike no hachisu kana* (*Shinsen Tsukubashū* 3720) ~In Buddhist allegory, the lotus—a plant with roots in the muddy water of the world whose pristine flowers open in the sky above—often represents hope for enlightenment.

Emperor Go-Tsuchimikado

117 *For a Sino-Japanese sequence composed at the palace on the ninth day of the Second Month of 1490*

A swallow flits by—
wind from its wings moving
my blinds.

118 *From a 100-verse sequence composed on the tenth day of the Ninth Month*

One chrysanthemum
left unpicked—home
to a butterfly.

119 *Composed for a monthly meeting at the imperial palace on the twenty-fifth day of the Tenth Month of 1484*

No wind in sight,
but fallen leaves
swirl beneath the trees.

1442–1500, r. 1464–1500.   Poet, patron of poets, and imperial sponsor of *Shinsen Tsukubashū.*

SPRING   (swallow) *Tsubame tobu hakaze ugokasu sudare kana* (Sanjōnishi Sanetaka, *Sanetaka-kō ki,* vol. 2, part 2, p. 393) ~Sino-Japanese sequence (*wakan renku*): a subgenre of linked verse with alternating Chinese and Japanese verses that was especially popular in Buddhist monasteries and among courtiers. ~The passing swallow offers a glimpse of balmier times to come. Sanetaka records that the emperor's hopes were unjustified: rain fell in coming days, followed by snow on the nineteenth. On that day, the emperor wrote another *hokku*: In chilling snow / yesterday's blossoms / are no more.

AUTUMN   (chrysanthemum) *Orinokosu kiku wa kochō no yadori kana* (*Shinsen Tsukubashū* 3776) ~The Chrysanthemum Banquet was held at the imperial palace yearly on the ninth day of the Ninth Month, following an ancient Chinese tradition. The flower was associated with longevity. The emperor's poem is therefore ironic in focusing on a flower left unpicked that has become home to a butterfly, a common metaphor for ephemerality.

AUTUMN   (fallen leaves) *Kaze miede ko no moto meguru ochiba kana* (*Shinsen Tsukubashū* 3811) ~With most trees now bare, the wind would not be visible—if not for fallen leaves lifted from the ground and blown about beneath the trees.

Ōuchi Masahiro

120 *From among his* hokku *on "Falling Blossoms"*

Blossoms scatter—
never knowing
our regrets.

121 *Composed on the twenty-fifth day of the Sixth Month of 1489*

Blow again—
and the closer the better,
autumn wind.

122 *For a linked-verse sequence composed during the Godless Month*

Autumn still remains—
in miscanthus plumes
on withered fields.

Inkō

123 *Composed in Echizen in the Tenth Month of 1515*

Morning showers
dangle from the moon
far and wide.

1446–1495.   Provincial warlord, poet, patron of the arts, and prime financial sponsor of *Shinsen Tsukubashū*.

SPRING   (scattering blossoms) *Chiru ya uki shiranu wa hana no kokoro kana* (*Shinsen Tsukubashū* 3672) ~How can the blossoms be so unfazed by their own demise?

AUTUMN   (autumn wind) *Fuke ya nao chikamasari suru aki no kaze* (*Shinsen Tsukubashū* 3728) ~The wind is a sign that autumn is on its way and, with it, relief from summer heat.

WINTER   (withered fields) *Aki wa nao susuki ni nokoru kareno kana* (*Shinsen Tsukubashū* 3806) ~Godless Month: the Tenth Month, called the Godless Month because of old legends about the various gods of shrines meeting at Izumo Shrine during that month, leaving the rest of the country "godless."

Died 1517.   Priest at Honkokuji (a Nichiren temple in Ōtsu, Ōmi Province [modern-day Shiga Prefecture]) and regional *renga* master.

AUTUMN   (showers, moon) *Asashigure tsuki yori kakaru chisato kana* (*Hokku kikigaki*, p. 11) ~Echizen: a province that is now the northern part of Fukui Prefecture, on the coast of the Sea of Japan.

124 *Composed at the Gateway at White River*

Fallen to the ground
like those words of old—
glowing leaves.

125 Dark spots
on hemp-white shore sand?
Plovers.

Shōhaku

126 *"Spring Moon"*

Where's the moon?
The haze-covered sky
is *all* light.

127 *A hokku requested by Sōseki after the death of Sōha*

Overwhelming
my memory—
blossoms at dusk.

AUTUMN (glowing leaves) *Chirishiku wa furu koto no ha no momiji kana* (*Shinsen Tsukubashū* 3808) ~Gateway at White River (Shirakawa no seki): an old checkpoint at the border between Shimotsuke Province and the far north, in modern-day Fukushima Prefecture. Of the many poems composed there ("words of old"), the one most relevant here is *SZS* 365, by Minamoto no Yorimasa (1104–1180): Back in the capital, / I saw only green leaves / all around, / but glowing leaves are strewn / on the ground at White River Gate.

WINTER (plovers) *Shirotae no masago no kuma ka hamachidori* (*Hokku kikigaki*, p. 10) ~From a distance, the spots look like gaps in the white sand—until they move. ~Hemp-white (*shirotae no*) is an ancient metaphoric epithet.

1443–1527. Member of the aristocratic Nakano'in lineage; student of Sōgi (p. 58); professional *renga* master who lived in Ikeda and later Izumi Sakai; and close friend of Sōchō (p. 80), Sanjōnishi Sanetaka (p. 90), and Sōseki (p. 94).

SPRING (haze) *Tsuki izuku sora wa kasumi no hikari kana* (*Ōtabon Shunmusōchū* 30) ~On a hazy night, the location of the moon is obscured, but its "backlighting" turns the whole sky white.

SPRING (blossoms) *Shinobu ni mo amaru wa hana no yūbe kana* (*Ōtabon Shunmusōchū* 111) ~Sōseki (p. 94). ~Sōha (d. 1512–1516): a disciple of Sōgi (p. 58). ~Compare *ShokuGSS* 1205, by Retired Emperor Juntoku (1197–1242, r. 1210–1221), about the imperial palace: In the stone-built palace / the old eaves are overgrown / with Memory Fern— / but ah, what a past is here, / still left to be remembered!

128 Beneath the eaves,
chatting on a rainy day—
barn swallows.

129 Summer rains—
mere trickles when falling
in thick forest.

130 Thunder showers
rain cool pearls
on oak groves.

131 In branches dense
with cicadas' drone—
one autumn leaf.

132 *Composed for a Sino-Japanese sequence*

Faint autumn light
falls on paulownia leaves.
Ah, for some rain!

133 *Composed for a memorial service for Sōgi, held at the home of Bishop
Shōei*

Words of old—
whispered today by wind
in the reeds.

SPRING   (barn swallows) *Ame no hi o kataru nokiba no tsubame kana* (*Ōtabon Shunmusōchū* 118) ~Swallows find some shelter under the eaves. The author of *Ōtabon Shunmusōchū*—which is generally attributed to Shōhaku's disciple Kawachiya Sōjin—notes that an old Chinese saying refers to spring swallows "talking about old times."

SUMMER   (summer rains) *Samidare mo shizuku ni otsuru miyama kana* (*Ōtabon Shunmusōchū* 190) ~Even in dense growth, strong summer showers break through—but only in trickles.

SUMMER   (thunder showers, cool) *Yūdachi no shiratama suzushi murakashiwa* (*Ōtabon Shunmusōchū* 208).

AUTUMN   (autumn leaf) *Semi no koe shigemi o aki no hitoha kana* (*Ōtabon Shunmusōchū* 232) ~One leaf signifies the arrival of autumn. Compare poem 10.

AUTUMN   (paulownia) *Kiri no ha ni aki no hi usushi ame mogana* (*Ōtabon Shunmusōchū* 236) ~Sino-Japanese sequence (*wakan renku*): a subgenre of linked verse with alternating Chinese and Japanese verses that was especially popular in Buddhist monasteries and among courtiers. ~The sunshine barely breaks through the dense paulownia foliage. Rain would bring both sound and color to the scene.

AUTUMN   (reeds) *Soyomeku ya kyō no furukoto ogi no koe* (*Ōtabon Shunmusōchū* 242) ~Sōgi (p. 58). ~Bishop Shōei: identity unknown. ~Compare *SKS* 146, by Koremune Takayori, about how "falling leaves have voices": When the wind blows, / the underleaves of the oak / make whispering sounds. / And where are they off to, / chatting as they go?

134   One wild-goose call—
      and even brighter shines
      the midnight moon.

135   *"Cricket"*

      Awake all night,
      the cricket never flagged—
      and now dawn.

136   *Composed at Yodo Village*

      In river mist—
      glowing leaves floating
      before they fall.

137   Is it so late?
      In moonlight, a stag calls
      out by gate paddies.

138   Awaiting whom?
      A mat of glowing leaves
      left by an evening gale.

139   *Composed at his hut*

      Not a sound,
      not even from leaves.
      My hut at dusk.

AUTUMN   (wild goose, moon) *Hitokoe ni sumu ya kari naku yowa no tsuki* (*Shinsen Tsukubashū* 3753) ~The sound of a wild goose calling—one of the chief indexes of the season—draws one's attention to another, the moon.

AUTUMN   (cricket) *Kirigirisu nenu yo o akanu asake kana* (*Ōtabon Shunmusōchū* 295) ~The cricket is awake all night, and so is the speaker.

AUTUMN   (mist, glowing leaves) *Kawagiri ni chirade mo ukabu momiji kana* (*Ōtabon Shunmusōchū* 317) ~Yodo Village: south of Kyoto in Fushimi, at the confluence of the Yodo, Kizu, and Katsura rivers. ~The mists rise so high that the leaves seem to float on the current.

AUTUMN   (stag) *Fukenuru ka tsuki ni shika naku kadota kana* (*Ōtabon Shunmusōchū* 323) ~Compare *SZS* 309, by Prince Sukehito (1073–1119): On an autumn night, / a stag calls and calls again / from the same peak, / but is closer / when the hour grows late. In Shōhaku's *hokku*, the stag has come much closer, down to the paddies near the gate.

AUTUMN   (glowing leaves) *Matsu ya tare momijimushiro no yūarashi* (*Ōtabon Shunmusōchū* 366) ~Compare *GSS* 1364, by Emperor Uda (867–931, r. 887–897): And if tonight / I were to make a sleep-mat / of autumn leaves— / would I still suffer / the heartaches of the road?

AUTUMN   (falling leaves) *Konoha sae oto senu io no yūbe kana* (*Ōtabon Shunmusōchū* 369) ~A line from a Chinese poem by Liu Changqing (709?–789?) reads, "Sheltered blossoms fall to earth, making not a sound." Shōhaku describes his own state as even more forlorn.

140 *For a 100-verse sequence in memory of Kensai*

Worldly fame:
jewels of hail, falling
in a dream.

141 *For a 1000-verse event sponsored by Masamori*

Dusk light
showing more has fallen?
A peak of snow.

Sakurai Motosuke

142 Pushed open
by the scent of plum—
morning's door.

143 In the mountains—rain.
Sunlight shining cool
at morning.

144 Blow, winds!
Colors will show brighter
on dead leaves below.

WINTER (hail) *Nadataru mo furu ya yume no ma tamaarare* (*Ōtabon Shunmusōchū* 395) ~Kensai: Inawashiro Kensai (p. 84). ~"Fame" translates the verb *nadatsu* (to stand high in reputation). Hail captures a moment's attention and then is gone. Here, though, coming down in a dream, it has no reality at all.

WINTER (snow) *Furisou to misuru ya yūbe yuki no mine* (*Shinsen Tsukubashū* 3841) ~Masamori: Fujiwara Masamori of Ikeda, a retainer of the Hosokawa clan who was Shōhaku's patron during his years in Ikeda.

Native of Settsu Province and disciple of Shinkei (p. 48) and later Sōgi (p. 58).

SPRING (plum blossoms) *Ume ga ka ni osarete hiraku asato kana* (Sakurai Motosuke, *Sakurai Motosuke shū* 1256) ~A breeze "opens" the night to morning with a scent that also brings the speaker to his door.

SUMMER (cool) *Yama ya ame teru hi suzushiki ashita kana* (Sakurai Motosuke, *Sakurai Motosuke shū* 1312) ~Summer weather is changeable, especially in the morning and the evening. Early light coming over the mountains is cool, thanks partly to the rain falling.

WINTER (dead leaves) *Fuke arashi shita wa iro koki kuchiba kana* (Sakurai Motosuke, *Sakurai Motosuke shū* 1284) ~The winds are sure to blow—and just now, that is all right, because the lower leaves of the tree will make a brighter spectacle on the ground.

Sōchō

145 *For a memorial service for Sōgi on the twenty-ninth day of the First Month of 1527*

An early spring—
sent back into seclusion
by morning snow.

146 The road home—
longer for all
after blossom viewing.

147 *Composed for a 100-verse sequence held on the fourth day of the Sixth Month of 1526*

For cicadas
the branches of a single tree
are a forest grove.

148 *Composed on the fifteenth day of the Sixth Month, when he was in Suruga*

In one day
snow melts to fall again—
cool on Fuji's peak.

149 *For a memorial service for Sōgi on the twenty-ninth day of the Seventh Month of 1523*

Bush clover, miscanthus—
in morning calm
after a storm.

1448–1532. A chief disciple and traveling companion of Sōgi (p. 58) and author of important journals and early comic *uta* and *renga*. After his master's death, he returned to his native East Country and worked as a professional *renga* master.

SPRING *Haru ya toki fuyugomorasuru asa no yuki* (Sōchō, *Sōchō shuki*, p. 116) ~Sōchō held memorial services for Sōgi on the twenty-ninth day of each month.

SPRING (blossom viewing) *Kaerusa wa tare mo tōyama sakuragari* (Sōchō, *Kabekusa* 2377) ~When going up the mountain to enjoy the blossoms, no one thinks of the road as long, but the same is not true when one must return home.

SUMMER (cicadas) *Hitomoto no kozue wa semi no hayashi kana* (Kidō, *Rengashi ronkō*, vol. 2, p. 945) ~Listening to the chorus of cicadas in a single tree makes one feel as if one is deep in the forest.

SUMMER (cool) *Kyō ni kiete furu yuki suzushi fuji no mine* (Sōchō, *Kabekusa* 2428) ~Suruga: modern-day Shizuoka Prefecture. ~Midday sun melts some snow on Fuji's peak, but more falls later, offering a cool sight to those suffering below in summer heat.

AUTUMN (bush clover, miscanthus) *Hagi susuki fukanu nowaki no ashita kana* (Sōchō, *Sōchō shuki*, p. 29) ~The calm symbolizes the repose of one who is finished with the storms of life.

150 *Composed at the residence of Mizuno Kisaburō, at a port called Toko-*
name in the Chita District

Morning moon—
the one boat left moored
in tideland pines.

151 A paulownia leaf
trembles in the wake
of morning rain.

152 Morning dew—
unfazed by that storm
last night.

153 *Composed for a 1000-verse event in the Ninth Month of 1526 at the home*
of Teramachi Saburōzaemon in Kyoto

Geese call out,
clearing the cold sky
at daybreak.

154 The work of showers?
Remnants of evening sun
on the autumn sea.

155 *Composed during the Godless Month, when he was visiting Koshi*

In Kyoto, never—
glowing leaves in the garden,
snow on the peaks.

AUTUMN (moon) *Tsuki ya kesa shiohi no matsu ni tomaribune* (Sōchō, *Nachigomori* 1683) ~Mizuno Kisaburō: a vassal of Mizuno Chikamori (d. 1556), one of Sōchō's chief patrons.

AUTUMN (paulownia) *Kiri no ha no ugoku ya nagori kesa no ame* (Sōchō, *Kabekusa* 2444).

AUTUMN (dew) *Asatsuyu wa sarigenaki yo no nowaki kana* (Sōchō, *Kabekusa* 2492).

AUTUMN (geese, cold sky) *Kari nakite samuki sora sumu ashita kana* (Sōchō, *Sōchō shuki*, p. 93) ~Teramachi Saburōzaemon: a retainer of the Hosokawa clan. ~Looking up after migrating geese call out, one feels autumn deepening in the clear cold of the sky.

AUTUMN (showers, autumn sea) *Shigureki ya yūhi o nokosu aki no umi* (Sōchō, *Kabekusa* 2503) ~Autumn showers are conventionally credited with dyeing leaves—but even the autumn sea?

AUTUMN (glowing leaves) *Miyako ya wa momiji no niwa ni mine no yuki* (*Shinsen Tsukubashū* 3826) ~Godless Month: the Tenth Month, called the Godless Month because of old legends about the various gods of shrines meeting at Izumo Shrine during that month, leaving the rest of the country "godless." ~Koshi: the ancient name for the Hokurikudō region, running along the Sea of Japan, from Wakasa to Echigo (roughly, modern-day Fukui to Niigata). ~To see autumn leaves in the garden and snow on the mountains in the Tenth Month would be rare in the capital, but snow falls earlier in the north.

156 *Composed when someone came from far in the east to visit him at his hut*

Come in—
my hut at least offers
shelter from rain.

157 Voices deepen
as garden fires flare white
in gusty wind.

Inawashiro Kensai

158 *Composed for a Sino-Japanese sequence at the home of Shinomiya Saemon no suke*

Beneath, ice thaws—
and last year's waters
begin to flow.

159 *Composed on the nineteenth day of the Third Month of 1492, at Shichijō Dōjō*

Blossoms scatter—
after hue and scent hinted
what was to come.

WINTER (rain) *Murashigure nurenu bakari no iori kana* (Sōchō, *Kabekusa* 2518) ~A self-effacing statement of welcome. One text says that the friend had come from Ueno Province (the northwestern part of modern-day Mie Prefecture).

WINTER (garden fires, gusty wind) *Koe fukeru niwabi ni shiroki arashi kana* (Sōchō, *Nachigomori* 2989) ~Kagura was a ritual form of dance involving masked dancers, performed outdoors at night by the light of *niwabi* (torches or standing fire cauldrons).

1452–1510. Disciple of Shinkei (p. 48) and later Sōgi (p. 58), whom he assisted in compiling *Shinsen Tsukubashū*, and professional *renga* master in the East Country.

SPRING (thawing ice) *Shita tokete kozo no mizu yuku kōri kana* (Inawashiro Kensai, *Sono no chiri*, p. 839) ~Sino-Japanese sequence (*wakan renku*): a subgenre of linked verse with alternating Chinese and Japanese verses that was especially popular in Buddhist monasteries and among courtiers. ~Shinomiya Saemon no Suke: Shinomiya Nagayoshi (d. 1504), a retainer of the Hosokawa clan.

SPRING (blossoms) *Hana zo chiru kakaramu tote no iroka kana* (*Shinsen Tsukubashū* 3666) ~Shichijō Dōjō: Kinkōji, a temple of the Time sect located near the intersection of Seventh Avenue and Hori Street in Kyoto. ~Kensai is quoted as saying that Emperor Go-Tsuchimikado (p. 68) declared this the finest *hokku* in *Shinsen Tsukubashū* (*Kensai zōdan*, p. 397).

160 *For a 100-verse sequence at the grave of Bishop Shinkei of the Jūjūshin'in in the spring of 1482*

In this world,
blossoms scatter, yes—
but do bloom again.

161 *On "Rice Seedlings"*

So small a paddy—
but with seedlings enough
for countless homes.

162 *Composed for a meeting held at Zōshūken*

Who knows why?
But cool somehow is the glow
of fireflies.

163 *Composed on the fifteenth day of the month*

Clouds, mist—
both hidden tonight
by the moon.

164 *Composed at Yanagizu Onzōji, in Aizu*

River mist—
and the sound of a boat
going by at dusk.

165 In bamboo groves,
the raucous sound
of hailstones.

SPRING (blossoms) *Chirinishi mo hana wa mata saku kono yo kana* (Inawashiro Kensai, *Sono no chiri*, p. 762) ~Bishop Shinkei (p. 48). ~Jūjūshin'in: a Tendai temple in Kyoto where Shinkei served as head priest before fleeing to the East Country.

SUMMER (rice seedlings) *Sebaki ta ni yadosu chisato no sanae kana* (Inawashiro Kensai, *Sono no chiri*, p. 771) ~A celebratory verse, expressing hope and gratitude for a rich harvest to come.

SUMMER (cool, fireflies) *Yue mo naku hikari suzushiki hotaru kana* (Inawashiro Kensai, *Sono no chiri*, p. 772) ~Zōshūken: one of the residences within Shōkokuji, a Zen temple in northern Kyoto. Both Sōgi (p. 58) and Kensai attended *renga* meetings there.

AUTUMN (moon) *Kumokiri mo tsuki ni kakururu koyoi kana* (*Shinsen Tsukubashū* 3765) ~So bright is the moon that it commands all attention.

AUTUMN (mist) *Kawakiri ya oto ni fune yuku yūbe kana* (Kaneko, *Rengashi Kensai denkō*, p. 182) ~Yanagizu Enzōji: a temple in Yanagizu, in Kensai's native Aizu (the western part of modern-day Fukushima Prefecture).

WINTER (hail) *Muratake ni koegoe moroshi tamaarare* (Inawashiro Kensai, *Sono no chiri*, p. 844).

166 *On the topic "Winter Moon," composed for a 1000-verse event held by the Yokose assistant in the Bureau of Court Music*

Of autumn fame,
but for light—ah, the moon
of a winter night.

167 A thin snowfall—
made deeper by moonlight
in the garden.

168 *From among his* hokku *composed at meetings in places around Shirakawa in 1497*

Water birds
push the moon about
in their sleep.

169 *On the topic "Snow in the Pines," composed for a 1000-verse event at the home of Lord Ōuchi, Master of the Left Capital*

Snowfall
on pines—a windless
blizzard.

170 *Composed in 1489 for a monthly meeting at the home of Lord Ōuchi, Master of the Left Capital*

Hawks take flight,
horses whinny—on a moor,
in a storm.

WINTER   (winter moon) *Na koso aki hikari wa fuyu no tsukiyo kana* (*Shinsen Tsukubashū* 3835) ~Yokose: Yokose Yasushige (1486–1545), a warrior and the governor of Shinano Province. ~Bureau of Court Music: the bureau at the imperial court in charge of *gagaku*, a musical form employed at court ceremonies. ~Sōgi (p. 58) is quoted as saying that he thought it unlikely that so fine a "moon" verse would ever be produced again (*Kensai zōdan*, p. 418).

WINTER   (snow, moon) *Usushi tote tsuki ni kasanaru niwa no yuki* (Sōgi, *Wakuraba* 2139) ~This *hokku* is recorded under the name Sōshun (the literary name the poet used until he changed it to Kensai at thirty-five years of age) in one of Sōgi's personal anthologies.

WINTER   (water birds) *Mizutori no tsuki o ugokasu ukine kana* (Inawashiro Kensai, *Sono no chiri*, p. 845) ~Shirakawa: Shirakawa no seki (Gateway at White River): an old checkpoint at the border between Shimotsuke Province and the far north, in modern-day Fukushima Prefecture.

WINTER   (snow, blizzard) *Matsu ni otsuru yuki wa kaze naki fubuki kana* (Inawashiro Kensai, *Sono no chiri*, p. 779) ~Lord Ōuchi: Ōuchi Masahiro (p. 70). ~When it gets heavy enough, snow on pine branches gives way, making a momentary blizzard.

WINTER   (hawks) *Taka tobai uma iwau no no arashi kana* (Inawashiro Kensai, *Sono no chiri*, p. 779) ~A hunting scene, captured in sights and sounds.

Sanjōnishi Sanetaka

171 *Composed on the fourth day of 1536*

Snow falls—
a memento from last year,
left by a cloud.

172 *For the first 100-verse sequence at the newly built cottage of Sōseki, on the
fourth day of the Fourth Month of 1523*

Not a speck of dust—
on the deutzia or the white
of the courtyard sand.

173 *For a meeting held by a monk from Suruga named Kenpo, on the twen-
ty-fourth day of the Fifth Month of 1528*

Chat about the snow
on Fuji's peak—
and summer is no more.

174 *Composed on the twenty-ninth day of the Seventh Month of 1528 for a
100-verse sequence in memory of Sōgi*

The sun beats down
but still autumn is here
in morning dew.

1455–1537. Court noble, poet, and scholar; student of Sōgi (p. 58) and confidant of Shōhaku (p. 72), Sōchō (p. 80), Inawashiro Kensai (p. 84), and Sōseki (p. 94); and prominent *uta* poet and participant in *renga* activities.

SPRING   (last year) *Yuki chirite furu toshi nokosu kumoi kana* (Sanjōnishi Sanetaka, *Saishōsō* addendum 1726) ~A conception similar to that in poem 158.

SUMMER   (deutzia) *Unohana ni chiri mo kumoranu masago kana* (Sanjōnishi Sanetaka, *Saishōsō* 4372) ~Sōseki (p. 94). ~In his diary, Sanetaka records a visit from Sōseki and Sōchō (p. 80) on the third, which he reciprocated the next day, braving a heavy rainstorm—perhaps what had washed the dust away—to do so.

SUMMER   *Fuji no ne no yuki o katareba natsu mo nashi* (Sanjōnishi Sanetaka, *Saishōsō* 5491) ~Suruga: the central part of modern-day Shizuoka Prefecture, which sits at the foot of Mount Fuji. ~Kenpo: identity unknown.

AUTUMN   (dew) *Teru hi ni mo izuku no aki zo kesa no tsuyu* (Sanjōnishi Sanetaka, *Saishōsō* 5519) ~Sōgi (p. 58) died, while journeying on the eastern seaboard, on the last day (actually, the thirtieth) of the Seventh Month of 1502. ~Dew, one of the chief symbols of autumn, is often a metaphor for tears and a symbol of transience.

175 *Composed at Maruyama in the Eastern Hills for a 1000-verse event held over three days, beginning on the tenth day of the Eighth Month of 1518*

Does the moon know—
that life is a morning glory
in the dark of night?

176 *For a 1000-verse event at Tenman Shrine on the twenty-third day of the Eighth Month of 1524 in Settsu Province, requested by Tadakata, Head of the Right Stables*

Blow in the pines—
maples are too fragile,
autumn winds!

177 *Composed rather casually for a short Sino-Japanese 100-verse sequence held by Reverend Jōan on the seventh day of the Tenth Month of 1533, when the time for Sokei's return to the provinces was approaching*

Showing kindness
to people on the road—
scattered showers.

AUTUMN (morning glory) *Tsuki ya shiru yo wa asagao no yo no ma kana* (Sanjōnishi Sanetaka, *Saishōsō* 3519) ~Maruyama: the location of Anrakuji, a temple of the Time sect in the Eastern Hills of the capital. The 1000-verse sequence was a votive offering to the temple to mark the third anniversary of the death of Nose Yorinori (d. 1516), a retainer of the Hosokawa clan who lived in Akutagawa, Settsu Province (the northern part of modern-day Osaka Prefecture).

AUTUMN (autumn winds) *Matsu o fuke momiji wa karoshi aki no kaze* (Sanjōnishi Sanetaka, *Saishōsō* 4701) ~Tenman Shrine: shrines dedicated to Sugawara no Michizane (845–903) were located in many provinces. ~Settsu Province: the western part of modern-day Hyōgō Prefecture. ~Tadakata: Hosokawa Tadakata (d. 1531). ~Sanetaka's diary records a visit from Tani Sōboku (p. 98) and another *renga* master on this day, but otherwise mentions only a stomachache and a fruitless visit from a physician.

AUTUMN (showers) *Yuku hito ni kokoro arikeri murashigure* (Sanjōnishi Sanetaka, *Saishōsō* addendum 1335) ~"Casually" translates *iisute no yō ni*. The men composed only a few verses, as a farewell gesture. ~Sino-Japanese sequence (*wakan renku*): a subgenre of linked verse with alternating Chinese and Japanese verses that was especially popular in Buddhist monasteries and among courtiers. ~Reverend Jōan: Jōan Ryōsu (d. 1536), the abbot of Ryōsen'in and the son of Tō no Tsuneyori (1401–1484), a warrior poet. ~Sokei: Jōan's nephew, a priest at the Saishō'in in Suruga, who had been studying under Sanetaka's direction since the autumn of the previous year. ~"Scattered" showers offer moments of respite along the road.

178 *For a 100-verse sequence at his house on the eleventh day of the Eleventh Month of 1515, when Sōchō came to visit*

All I waited for:
blossoms, glowing leaves,
then this morning—snow.

179 *Composed on the twenty-fifth day of the Twelfth Month of 1519*

Piled up
against the New Year—
snow at dusk.

Sōseki

180 High tide
breaks up the ice
at shoreline.

181 *For a meeting held in Sasaya in Kyoto*

Winds blow,
tying and untying fronds
of willow trees.

182 Spring departs—
the clear moon oblivious
of passing time.

WINTER   (snow) *Machikoshi ya hana ni momiji ni kesa no yuki*
(Sanjōnishi Sanetaka, *Saishōsō* 2953) ~Sōchō (p. 80). ~A tour de force
that comprehends an entire year in its 17 syllables. Sanetaka's diary re-
cords that snow did indeed fall that day.

WINTER   (snow) *Tsumorikeri toshi o arasou yuki no kure* (Sanjōnishi
Sanetaka, *Saishōsō* 3732) ~Spring begins with the New Year, but here
winter snow contests the issue. ~Sanetaka's diary notes snow falling on
the twenty-fourth.

1474–1533.   Disciple and heir of Sōgi's (p. 58) *renga* practice in Kyoto
who likewise traveled widely through the provinces to visit patrons while
maintaining close ties with men such as Sanjōnishi Sanetaka (p. 90) in
the Home Provinces.

SPRING   (ice breaking up) *Mitsu shio no kōri o kudaku migiwa kana*
(*Nikonshū*, vol. 2, p. 84) ~A scene of early spring.

SPRING   (willows) *Fukimusubi fukitoku kaze no yanagi kana* (*Hokkuchō*,
p. 47) ~Sasaya: an area in northern Kyoto.

SPRING   *Haru zo yuku omoi kuma naki tsukihi kana* (*Nikonshū*, vol. 2,
p. 128) ~A rare "abstract" statement concerning the constant passage of
time, although the sentiment expressed is traditional in the way it focuses
on the gap between the natural and human worlds.

183 *Composed in the Eighth Month of 1522, as the fifth* hokku *for a 1000-verse event at Ise*

Going deep,
I leave summer behind
on the mountain path.

184 *Composed at Miidera*

Moon out at dusk—
and just a bit of lake
between the trees.

185 *Composed in the Eleventh Month of 1521, as the second* hokku *for a 1000-verse event offered to Sumiyoshi Shrine*

Night showers—
and before the sky is dry,
morning sun.

186 *Composed at Chōkōji in Ōmi, at the age of nineteen*

A bell, alone—
on a snowy evening,
below a mountain.

SUMMER   *Fukaku irite natsu o okurasu yamaji kana* (Sōchō and Sōseki, *Ise senku*) ~Ise: the eastern part of modern-day Mie Prefecture and the site of Ise Shrine, dedicated to the Sun Goddess. *Ise senku* was composed by Sōchō (p. 80) and Sōseki over five days, as a votive offering for Hosokawa Takakuni (1484–1531) on the eve of battle. The topic of this *hokku* was "Escaping the Heat." ~Compare *SZS* 1278, by Saigyō (1118–1190), written when he was living in a mountain temple at Futaminoura, near Ise: Going deep, / I enter the pathway / of the god— / where transcendent, above all, / is the wind in the pines.

AUTUMN   (moon) *Yūzukuyo umi sukoshi aru ko no ma kana* (*Hokkuchō*, p. 252) ~Miidera: the colloquial name of Onjōji, the great Tendai temple in Ōtsu, on the southern shore of Lake Biwa.

WINTER   (showers) *Sayoshigure sora mo hinu ma no asahi kana* (Kidō, *Rengashi ronkō*, vol. 2, p. 941) ~Sumiyoshi Shrine: a Shinto shrine located between Naniwa and Sakai, dedicated to Sumiyoshi Daimyōjin, patron god of poets. The 1000-verse sequence—known as *Sumiyoshi senku*— was produced by Sōseki and Sanjōnishi Sanetaka (p. 90) and presented to the shrine as a votive offering.

WINTER   (snow) *Kane hitori yuki no yūbe no fumoto kana* (*Nikonshū*, vol. 2, p. 75) ~Chōkōji: a temple in the vicinity of Ōmi Hachiman, in modern-day Shiga Prefecture. ~Sōseki's personification of the word "bell" with the word "alone" (meaning, literally, "one person" in Japanese) is unusual.

Reizei Tamekazu

187 *Composed as a proxy for Takeda Harunobu on the third day of the Third Month of 1542, in Suruga*

Blossoms fall
and morning wind is white
beneath the trees.

188 *Composed by request, in the Sixth Month of 1521, in Kyoto*

That sound of thunder
storming at my eaves—
was hailstones.

189 *Composed at Nanao in Noto for a 1000-verse event on the twenty-fifth day of the Fifth Month of 1526, as a proxy for the second son of Hatakeyama Saemon no Suke*

How long the night
when it appears at dusk—
summer moon.

Tani Sōboku

190 *Composed for the second 100-verse sequence of a 1000-verse event held at his cottage between the thirteenth and fifteenth days of the Second Month*

Far-flowing water—
and wild geese sent off
by swaying willows.

1486–1549. Heir of a court poetic lineage who spent a great deal of time in the provinces because of financial exigencies.

SPRING   (blossoms) *Hana ochite asakaze shiroki kokage kana* (Reizei Tamekazu, *Tamekazu shū* 1868) ~Takeda Harunobu (Shingen, 1521–1573): one of the greatest warlords of the pre-Edo period. After Shingen overthrew the Imagawa, Tamekazu's erstwhile patrons, in 1541, Tamekazu was a fixture at Shingen's literary events.

SUMMER   (thunder) *Yūdachi no oto wa nokiba no arare kana* (Reizei Tamekazu, *Tamekazu shū* 588) ~From his middle age onward, Tamekazu spent much of his time in the provinces, but in 1521 he was in Kyoto, attending court events, holding his own poetry gatherings, and providing services to his patrons.

SUMMER   (summer moon) *Yūbe yori idete yo nagashi natsu no tsuki* (Reizei Tamekazu, *Tamekazu shū* 1265) ~Nanao: a stronghold in Noto Province. ~Hatakeyama Saemon no Suke: Hatakeyama Yoshifusa (1491–1545), the warlord of Noto. The Reizei had many disciples in the area and visited there often.

Died 1545.   Disciple of Sōchō (p. 80) and Sōseki (p. 94) who spent a long life as a *renga* master, active both in the Kyoto area and in the provinces.

SPRING   (willows) *Mizu tōki karigane okuru yanagi kana* (Tani Sōboku, *Kochiku* 26) ~In *Kochiku*, an unidentified disciple notes that the verse garnered high praise from Sōboku's aristocratic friends in the capital. ~Wild geese fly off to summer in the north.

191   *Composed at Utsunomiya in 1545*

A tangle of light:
fireflies protesting
against my fan.

192   *Composed in 1545 for a meeting at the home of Zen'a in Sano*

Motionless
mountain water, clear—
in an autumn garden.

193   *For the monthly meeting of Lord Hosokawa, governor of Harima*

Hawks at the hunt
amid snow flurries
of miscanthus.

194   Gathering clouds
cannot contain the moonlight
in hailstones.

195   Rain—and snow
still there on far mountains
at dusk.

196   And had he been out?
Still I would hate to leave
his snowy home.

SUMMER   (fireflies, fan) *Uttae ni hotaru midaruru ōgi kana* (Tani Sōboku, *Kanazawa kushū* 52) ~Utsunomiya: in modern-day Tochigi Prefecture, one of the places the poet visited on his last journey.

AUTUMN   (autumn garden) *Ugoki naki yamamizu kiyoshi aki no niwa* (Tani Sōboku, *Kanazawa kushū* 59) ~ Zen'a: a priest, otherwise unidentified. ~It was just a short time after writing this *hokku* that Sōboku died, in Sano (Shimotsuke Province), on the twenty-second day of the Ninth Month of 1545.

WINTER   (hawks, snow) *Kotakagari chirikau yuki ya hanasusuki* (Tani Sōboku, *Kochiku* 11) ~Lord Hosokawa: Hosokawa Mototsune (d. 1554), the adoptive father of Hosokawa Yūsai (p. 122).

WINTER   (hail) *Murakumo ni tsuki mo tamaranu arare kana* (Tani Sōboku, *Kochiku* 38).

WINTER   (snow) *Ame ya yuki tōyama nokoru yūbe kana* (Tani Sōboku, *Kochiku* 39) ~Kochiku says that this verse must have been composed in Kyoto, probably because of a perceived allusion to *ShokuKKS* 639, by Fujiwara no Teika (1162–1241): Cold builds / in the capital, but still / no snowflakes fall— / though the peaks are white / out beyond the evening rain.

WINTER   (snow) *Awade sae kaerusa oshiki yuki no yado* (*Nikonshū*, vol. 2, p. 117) ~Again, the triumph of the aesthetic over the practical. Leaving his friend behind is painful enough—more so when snow has beautified his hut.

Shūkei

197 High peaks above—
and a great river brimming
with last year's snow.

198 A lark calls,
and for colts in the field—
no more flowers.

199 *Composed for the fourth 100-verse sequence of a 1000-verse event held in 1544*

Falling onto moss
they glow again below—
autumn leaves.

Sōyō

200 Summer rains
plant mountain paddies
with clouds.

201 Bringing the moon
through my door of black pine:
a water rail.

Died 1544. Disciple of Sōseki (p. 94) and teacher of Satomura Jōha (p. 114).

SPRING (last year) *Mine takaki ōkawamizu ya kozo no yuki* (*Hokkuchō,* p. 40).

SPRING (lark) *Hibari naku nobe no murakoma hana mo nashi* (*Hokkuchō,* p. 108) ~Larks rise high above a field, distracting colts from grazing for a moment.

AUTUMN (autumn leaves) *Chirite nao koke no shitateru momiji kana* (Kidō, *Rengashi ronkō,* vol. 2, p. 956) ~Fallen leaves take on more vibrant colors against a backdrop of green moss.

Died 1563. Son and heir of Tani Sōboku (p. 98) who was active in both noble and warrior circles and was particularly favored by the warlord Miyoshi Chōkei (p. 112).

SUMMER (summer rains) *Samidare wa kumo o uetaru yamada kana* (*Hokkuchō,* p. 163) ~After showers pass, fresh water in the paddies reflects scattered clouds overhead.

SUMMER (water rail) *Maki no to ni tsuki o iretaru kuina kana* (*Hokkuchō,* p. 174) ~The call of the water rail is often compared to a "knocking" sound—here ushering in moonlight when the resident of the house opens his door.

202 This is autumn:
snipes rising from marshes
at evening.

203 *Composed on the sixth day of the Eleventh Month of 1563 for a 100-verse*
event held by Miyoshi Chōkei at Iimori Castle, Kawachi Province

In mountain scrub,
the rustle of evening
showers.

204 In a flowing stream—
leaves weighed down
with light snow.

205 Moonbeams
cross over thin ice—
yet don't get wet.

206 Frozen over?
Beach plovers walking
on the water.

Arakida Moritake

207 In spring rain
bird calls darken, mountains
are no more.

AUTUMN   *Aki wa tada shigi tatsu sawa no yūbe kana* (*Hokkuchō*, p. 268)
~Compare *SKKS* 362, by Saigyō (1118–1190): Even one who claims / to
be beyond feeling / is moved by this somber beauty: / snipes rising from
a swamp / on an autumn evening.

AUTUMN   (showers) *Yamashiba ni yūhi soyomeku shigure kana*
(*Hokkuchō*, p. 304) ~Miyoshi Chōkei (p. 112). ~Iimori Castle: a mountain fortress in Kawachi Province (the eastern part of modern-day Osaka
Prefecture).

WINTER   (snow) *Yuku mizu ni usuyuki omoki ochiba kana* (*Hokkuchō*,
p. 314).

WINTER   (ice) *Kage ya tsuki wataredo nurenu usukōri* (Kidō, *Rengashi
ronkō*, vol. 2, p. 759).

WINTER   (frozen, plovers) *Kōriki ya mizu no ue yuku hamachidori*
(*Hokkuchō*, p. 357).

1473–1549.   Heir of a priestly family associated with Ise Shrine; *uta* poet
and *renga* master who participated in sessions with Sōgi (p. 58), Shōhaku
(p. 72), Sōchō (p. 80), Inawashiro Kensai (p. 84), Sōseki (p. 94), and
Tani Sōboku (p. 98); and known for his *haikai*.

SPRING   (spring rain) *Harusame ni tori no ne kurete yama mo nashi*
(*Hōraku hokku shū* 128).

208 *Composed for the first 100-verse sequence of a solo 1000-verse event held*
in memory of Sōchō on the twenty-fifth day of the Third Month of 1532

The morning after
"a spring night dream"—
that feeling.

209 How many days
since these rains began?
Fifth Month.

210 A far island
bobs on blighted leaves
in the reeds.

211 More colorful
for being trod upon—
rotting leaves.

Shōkyū

212 There, I see it,
that same gap in the mist—
but no Nagara Mountain.

SPRING   (spring night) *Haru no yo no yume no ashita no kokoro kana*
(Kidō, *Rengashi ronkō*, vol. 2, p. 950) ~Sōchō (p. 80) had died on the sixth
day of the month. ~Spring night dreams were conventionally fleeting and
insubstantial, leaving the dreamer with a vague feeling of loss. Compare
SKKS 38, by Fujiwara no Teika (1162–1241): The floating bridge / of my
spring night dream / has broken away: / and lifting off a far peak— / a
cloudbank trailing in the sky.

SUMMER   (Fifth Month) *Furisomeshi ame itsu no hi no satsuki kana*
(*Hōraku hokku shū* 427) ~Even after a few days, the summer rains seem
endless.

WINTER   (blighted leaves) *Tōshima wa kareha ni ukabu ashibe kana*
(*Hōraku hokku shū* 1007).

WINTER   (rotting leaves) *Fumiwakeshi ato wa iro koki kuchiba kana*
(*Hōraku hokku shū* 1118) ~Someone tramping through the leaves turns
up a little remaining color.

Died 1552.   Disciple of Tani Sōboku (p. 98) and founder of the Sato-
mura lineage of *renga* poets, which would be a major force in *renga* circles
throughout the Edo period.

AUTUMN   (mist) *Mireba mishi kirima nagara no yama mo nashi*
(*Hokkuchō*, p. 233) ~Nagara Mountain: in Shiga Prefecture, behind Mi-
idera temple. ~The mountain, of course, is still there; it is the mist that
has moved.

213 Colder even
than the wind's sound—
the midnight moon.

214 Mountain winds
bring a break in the snow—
filled by hail.

Ikkadō Jōa

215 Fireflies flying
in gaps between branches—
a grove of stars.

216 *For a meeting held in Musashi by Narita, governor of Shimōsa*

In the treetops,
cicadas exchange words—
partners in poetry.

217 *Composed on the day after a typhoon*

Leaves on the reeds
will be suffering too—
after a storm.

WINTER (cold) *Fuku kaze no oto yori samushi yowa no tsuki* (*Hokkuchō*, p. 323).

WINTER (snow, hail) *Yamakaze no yuki no todae no arare kana* (*Hokkuchō*, p. 332).

1501–1562. Born into the Hatakeyama house, head priest of the Ikkadō in Sunpu (a temple of the Time sect) and later twenty-ninth head of that sect, friend of Tani Sōboku (p. 98), and frequent participant in *renga* events throughout the East Country.

SUMMER (fireflies) *Ko no ma yuku hotaru wa hoshi no hayashi kana* (Ikkadō Jōa, *Sekitai* 280).

SUMMER (cicadas) *Koe kawasu kozue no semi ya uta no tomo* (Ikkadō Jōa, *Sekitai* 300) ~Musashi: a province that makes up most of modern-day Saitama Prefecture. ~Narita, governor of Shimōsa: the Narita were longtime warlords in Musashi.

AUTUMN (reeds, storm) *Ogi no ha mo kurushikaru ran nowaki kana* (Ikkadō Jōa, *Sekitai* 306) ~Poems about reeds in the wind usually focus on sound. This one personifies the plants, imagining that they, too, have suffered damage in a storm.

218   *Composed at the ruins in Fujisawa, Sagami Province*

Many-hued grasses—
glowing in memory
of flowery fields.

219   *Composed at Mito, in Rikuzen*

Ducks forage
on morning ice
in barren fields.

Sanjōnishi Kin'eda

220   *Composed for a 100-verse sequence on the twenty-third day of the Seventh Month of 1563*

Does it not know
about the wind?
Morning dew on bush clover.

221   *Composed for the tenth 100-verse sequence of a 1000-verse Sino-Japanese event held at Daikakujidono on the twenty-third day of the Eighth Month of 1556*

The clouds rain—
and the rains stay on
in autumn trees.

AUTUMN   (glowing grasses) *Irokusa no momiji ni nokoru hanano kana* (Ikkadō Jōa, *Sekitai* 333) ~Fujisawa: the site of Yūgyōji, the traditional headquarters of the Time sect. The temple burned in 1513 and was not rebuilt until 1607, during which time the Ikkadō served as the headquarters of the sect. ~"Flowery fields" is a metaphor for the look of the place in happier times.

WINTER   (ice) *Ashigamo ya kareno ni asaru asakōri* (Ikkadō Jōa, *Sekitai* 356) ~Mito: a castle town in Hitachi Province (modern-day Ibaraki Prefecture).

1487–1563.   Second son of Sanjōnishi Sanetaka (p. 90) and major poetic and scholarly figure in his own right.

AUTUMN   (bush clover) *Kaze ari to shirazu ya hagi ni kesa no tsuyu* (Kidō, *Rengashi ronkō*, vol. 2, p. 971).

AUTUMN   (autumn trees) *Kumo ya shiguru shigure wa tomaru kigi no aki* (Kidō, *Rengashi ronkō*, vol. 2, p. 966) ~Sino-Japanese sequence (*wakan renku*): a subgenre of linked verse with alternating Chinese and Japanese verses that was especially popular in Buddhist monasteries and among courtiers. ~Daikakujidono: an imperial residence in the Saga area, west of Kyoto.

222 *Composed for the tenth 100-verse sequence in a 1000-verse event held in Kyoto by Ōuchi Yoshitaka on the eleventh day of the Fifth Month of 1551*

On top of frost,
the splendor of snow
in pine wind.

Miyoshi Chōkei

223 *Composed on the twenty-sixth day of the Second Month of 1554 for a memorial service for Jūkei*

A hazy night—
and somewhere out there,
the absent moon.

224 *Composed on the twenty-second day of the Ninth Month of 1551 for a 100-verse memorial sequence on the seventh anniversary of Sōboku's death*

Yearning after leaves
gone on autumn wind—
rain showers.

225 *Composed in 1563*

A dusting of snow—
and I forget about blossoms
on withered fields.

WINTER (frost, snow) *Shimo no ue ya yuki mo itsukushi matsu no kaze* (Kidō, *Rengashi ronkō*, vol. 2, p. 961) ~Ōuchi Yoshitaka (1507–1551): a great warlord and a patron of artists.

Died 1564. Vassal of the Hosokawa clan who overthrew the leader of that clan, becoming one of the most powerful warlords, and student of Sōyō (p. 102) and Shōkyū (p. 106).

SPRING (haze) *Kasumu yo wa munashiki tsuki no yukue kana* (Kawazoe, Tanamachi, and Shimazu, eds., *Dazaifu Tenmangū rengashi*, vol. 2, p. 301) ~Jūkei (d. after 1552): a calligrapher and scribe who went on to become a prominent *renga* poet. Sōyō (p. 102) and Satomura Jōha (p. 114) also participated in the sequence honoring his memory.

AUTUMN (autumn leaves, showers) *Aki no ha no chiru ato shinobu shigure kana* (Kidō, *Rengashi ronkō*, vol. 2, p. 961) ~Sōboku: Tani Sōboku (p. 98) died in 1545.

WINTER (snow) *Usuyuki ni hana mo omowanu kareno kana* (Kidō, *Rengashi ronkō*, vol. 2, p. 972).

226 *Composed on the tenth day of the Twelfth Month of 1560*

Even on mountains
that aren't truly mountains:
deep morning snow.

Satomura Jōha

227 *For the third 100-verse sequence of a 1000-verse event on the fifth day of*
the Second Month of 1571 at Ōharano, sponsored by Hosokawa Yūsai

Ah, for some pain—
to make me forget about
the moon, blossoms.

228 *Composed at Zenrinji*

For a heart serene
there is no scattering
of blossoms.

229 One cherry tree—
a tollgate for people
from near and far.

230 *Composed for the third 100-verse sequence of* Mōri senku

Wind in blossoms—
the sound of an axe
cutting firewood.

WINTER   (snow) *Yama naranu yama sae kesa wa miyuki kana* (Kidō, *Rengashi ronkō*, vol. 2, p. 969).

1524–1602.   Heir of the Satomura lineage of *renga* poets, professional *renga* master, and author of numerous handbooks and treatises.

SPRING   (blossoms) *Tsuki hana ni wasuru bakari no usa mogana* (Satomura Jōha, *Jōha hokkuchō* 339) ~Ōharano: an area southwest of Kyoto. ~Hosokawa Yūsai (p. 122) ~Compare *GSIS* 573, by Izumi Shikibu (fl. 970–1030), written after the death of Prince Atsumichi: Now that he is gone, / how I wish I could recall / "That time, yes, that time!"— / some painful time / to make me want to forget!

SPRING   (blossoms) *Shizuka naru kokoro ni wa chiru hana mo nashi* (Satomura Jōha, *Jōha hokkuchō* 404) ~Zenrinji: Eikandō Zenrinji, headquarters of the Seizan branch of the Pure Land sect of Buddhism, located just north of Nanzenji in the Eastern Hills of Kyoto.

SPRING   (cherry tree) *Hana hitoki ochikochibito no sekiji kana* (Satomura Jōha, *Jōha hokkuchō* 418) ~Passersby cannot help but stop to admire the blossoms.

SPRING   (blossoms) *Hana ni fuku kaze ya somagi no ono no oto* (Satomura Jōha, *Jōha hokkuchō* 475) ~*Mōri senku*: a 1000-verse duo sequence by Jōha and Satomura Shōshitsu (p. 118), composed from the twelfth to the sixteenth day of the Fifth Month of 1594. Commissioned by Mōri Terumoto (1523–1625), it celebrated the completion of a 10,000-verse votive sequence presented by the Mōri to Itsukushima Shrine.

231 *Composed for a 100-verse sequence on the topic "Reminiscence" on the twenty-second day of the Fourth Month of 1587*

What's that, cuckoo?
"Stay awake!" you say—
to muse on the past?

232 *Composed for a 100-verse sequence on the fourth day of the Seventh Month of 1574, when Uji Bridge had been rebuilt*

A plank bridge
of black pine goes white
in evening moonlight.

233 *Composed for the seventh 100-verse sequence of* Mōri senku

Moon at daybreak—
mountains no longer there
at a field's far edge.

234 *For the second 100-verse sequence of a 1000-verse event sponsored by Akechi Mitsuhide on the nineteenth day of the Eleventh Month of 1581*

Year round,
one thing doesn't change—
the moon in the sky.

SUMMER   (cuckoo) *Mukashi omou nezame seyo to ka hototogisu* (Satomura Jōha, *Jōha hokkuchō* 695) ~Compare *SKKS* 201, by Fujiwara no Shunzei (1114–1204): Musing on the past, / I sit in my hut of grass / amid night showers. / Must you add my tears to the rain, / you cuckoo of the mountain?

AUTUMN   (moon) *Maki no ita no tsugihashi shiroshi tsukuyo kana* (Satomura Jōha, *Jōha hokkuchō* 1211) ~Uji Bridge: a famous bridge over the Uji River, south of the capital.

AUTUMN   (moon) *Akete tsuki ochikatanobe wa yama mo nashi* (Satomura Jōha, *Jōha hokkuchō* 1229) ~*Mōri senku*: a 1000-verse duo sequence by Jōha and Satomura Shōshitsu (p. 118), composed from the twelfth to the sixteenth day of the Fifth Month of 1594. Commissioned by Mōri Terumoto (1523–1625), it celebrated the completion of a 10,000-verse votive sequence presented by the Mōri to Itsukushima Shrine.

AUTUMN   (moon) *Toshi no uchi ni kawaranu ya tada sora no tsuki* (Satomura Jōha, *Jōha hokkuchō* 1267) ~Akechi Mitsuhide (1528–1582): one of the great warlords of the day. ~Compare *FGS* 1683, by Kyōgoku Tameko (d. 1316): When the time comes, / blossoms and autumn leaves / have their glory days. / But how moving it is / that the moon never changes!

235 *Composed for a solo 1000-verse sequence honoring the twenty-seventh-day services for Sanjōnishi Kin'eda in the Twelfth Month of 1563*

On Saga's slope,
snowfall leaves no trace
of the ancient path.

Satomura Shōshitsu

236 *Composed for a solo 100-verse sequence in the First Month of 1587*

Yearly, my plum trees
are evergreens—
of a different hue.

237 *Composed for a 100-verse sequence at the Jurakutei Palace of Toyotomi Hidetsugu on the ninth day of the Third Month of 1593*

What are cherries
after their time has gone?
Trees in rows.

238 Summer rains come
and the cove's tidal flats
are never dry.

239 *A prayer for someone going off on a journey*

This coolness—
a guide for the one
coming to visit.

WINTER   (snow) *Saga no yama yuki no furumichi ato mo nashi* (Satomura Jōha, *Jōha hokkuchō* 1599) ~Sanjōnishi Kin'eda (p. 110). ~Saga: an area just west of Kyoto. The grave markers of Sanetaka (p. 90), Kin'eda, and other members of the Sanjōnishi family are on the mountainside behind Nison'in Temple in Saga. ~Compare *GSS* 1075, by Ariwara no Yukihira (818–893), composed when visiting the site of an imperial progress of decades before: At Seri River, / where my Lord tarried / now so long ago, / still there are signs / of the ancient path.

Died 1603.   Son and heir of Shōkyū (p. 106), founder of the Satomura lineage of *renga* poets, and disciple of Satomura Jōha (p. 114), who married him to his daughter and made Shōshitsu his heir.

SPRING   (plum trees) *Toshigoto no iro ya tokiwagi yado no ume* (Kidō, *Rengashi ronkō*, vol. 2, p. 988).

SPRING   (cherries) *Toki arite saku to mo hana wa namiki kana* (*Hokkuchō*, p. 94) ~Jurakutei Palace: the grand palace erected in central Kyoto by Toyotomi Hideyoshi (1536–1598) in the late 1580s. ~Toyotomi Hidetsugu (1568–1595): Hideyoshi's nephew and—for a brief time—his heir and successor.

SUMMER   (summer rains) *Samidare wa shiohi mo shiranu irie kana* (*Hokkuchō*, p. 165).

SUMMER   (coolness) *Suzushisa wa ima kon hito no shirube kana* (*Hokkuchō*, p. 192).

240 After the wind,
   rain strikes leaves fallen
   from the paulownias.

241 *Composed for the eighth 100-verse sequence of* Mōri senku

   Of those lights
   sparkling in the ripples—
   which is *the* moon?

242 Cease now, showers—
   the leaves of richest color
   are sure to fall.

243 *For the seventh 100-verse sequence of a 1000-verse event sponsored by
   Akechi Mitsuhide on the nineteenth day of the Eleventh Month of 1581*

   On the mountains,
   even out on a sandspit—
   deep morning snow.

Oka Kōsetsu

244 More haze
   than the sky could hold?
   Today's rain.

AUTUMN (paulownias) *Kaze taete ame kiku kiri no ochiba kana* (*Hokkuchō*, p. 222) ~In the quiet after the wind stops blowing, one can hear the patter of rain on newly fallen leaves.

AUTUMN (moon) *Sese ni sumu kage wa izure ka sora no tsuki* (*Hokkuchō*, p. 258) ~*Mōri senku*: a 1000-verse duo sequence by Satomura Jōha (p. 114) and Shōshitsu, composed from the twelfth to the sixteenth day of the Fifth Month of 1594. Commissioned by Mōri Terumoto (1523–1625), it celebrated the completion of a 10,000-verse votive sequence presented by the Mōri to Itsukushima Shrine.

AUTUMN (showers, autumn leaves) *Somenokose iro koki wa chiru momiji kana* (*Hokkuchō*, p. 285).

WINTER (snow) *Yama mo isa shirasu ni fukashi kesa no yuki* (Kidō, *Rengashi ronkō*, vol. 2, p. 984) ~Akechi Mitsuhide (1528–1582): one of the great warlords of the day.

Died 1609. Samurai in service to the Hōjō of Odawara and later Toyotomi Hideyoshi (1536–1598) and Tokugawa Ieyasu (1543–1616) who was highly respected as both an *uta* and a *renga* poet.

SPRING (haze) *Kasumi yori kumiamasu sora ka kyō no ame* (Oka Kōsetsu, *Kōsetsu eisō* 531).

245 Wind on board,
     a sailboat makes its way
     on spring seas.

246 *For a memorial service*

     No grieving!
     Our waking world, too,
     is a spring dream.

247 Fire sparked
     by rain striking stone?
     Rock azaleas.

248 Wind and waves
     chide any who would sleep
     on a moonlit night.

Hosokawa Yūsai

249 *Composed at Omoigawa during a journey through Kyūshū in 1587*

     As darkness falls,
     fireflies guide us along
     Longing River.

SPRING   (spring seas) *Kaze o nosete maho yuku fune ya haru no umi*
(Oka Kōsetsu, *Kōsetsu eisō* 551) ~Compare *SCSS* 16, by Princess Shokushi
(d. 1201): On the Sea of Grebes, / a boat rows along / beyond the haze—
/ its sails billowing forth / to make a vista of spring.

SPRING   (spring dream) *Uramu na yo samenokoru yo mo haru no yume*
(Oka Kōsetsu, *Kōsetsu eisō* 555) ~Excessive grieving may indicate too
great an attachment to the world.

SPRING   (rock azaleas) *Ame no utsu ishi no hi ka moyuru iwatsutsuji*
(Oka Kōsetsu, *Kōsetsu eisō* 563).

AUTUMN   (moon) *Namikaze wa tsuki ni nuru yo no isame kana* (Oka
Kōsetsu, *Kōsetsu eisō* 572).

1534–1610.   Son of one of the last Ashikaga shoguns who was taken in as
heir to the Hosokawa lineage and became a powerful warlord, disciple of
Sanjōnishi Saneki (1511–1579), and *uta* poet.

SUMMER   (fireflies) *Kururu yo no hotaru ya shirube omoigawa* (Hoso-
kawa Yūsai, *Kyūshū no michi no ki*, p. 557) ~Omoigawa (Longing River):
a river that runs through Dazaifu, then the chief city of northern Kyūshū.
~This *hokku* was composed when Yūsai accompanied Toyotomi Hideyo-
shi (1536–1598) on his campaign in Kyūshū, the more literary facets of
which are recorded in Yūsai's *Kyūshū no michi no ki*.

250 *Composed upon request from the steward of Tsushima during the Sixth Month of 1587*

Rising high
among distant islands—
pinnacles of cloud.

251 *Composed for a 100-verse sequence in memory of Oda Nobunaga, on the fifteenth day of the Seventh Month of 1582*

Reminders:
ink-dyed robes at dusk,
dew on our sleeves.

252 *Composed while on campaign in the East Country in the Seventh Month of 1590, at Kōfu, on the request of Unsai Sōju*

Ah, for winds—
to blow clouds and mist
from the mountain moon.

253 *Composed upon request while on campaign in Kyūshū on the eighteenth day of the Seventh Month of 1587*

The moon's charms—
a rope to keep us moored
in harbor.

SUMMER   (pinnacles of cloud) *Tōshima ni tachikuwawaru ya kumo no mine* (Hosokawa Yūsai, *Kyūshū no michi no ki*, p. 561) ~Tsushima: an island in the northern part of modern-day Nagasaki Prefecture. ~This *hokku* was also composed during Hideyoshi's campaign in Kyūshū. ~"Pinnacles of cloud" (*kumo no mine*) is a metaphor that refers to clouds rising into the sky to form peaks.

AUTUMN   (dew) *Sumizome no yūbe ya nagori sode no tsuyu* (Kidō, *Rengashi ronkō*, vol. 2, p. 985) ~Oda Nobunaga (1534–1582): a great warlord whom Yūsai served. He was betrayed by his own vassals and obliged to commit suicide at Honnōji in Kyoto on the second day of the Sixth Month of 1582. Yūsai convened a *renga* meeting in his honor in a makeshift shelter built on the ashes of the burned-out temple in which Satomura Jōha (p. 114) and a number of court aristocrats participated.

AUTUMN   (mist, moon) *Kumokiri ni tsuki no yama kosu kaze mogana* (Hosokawa Yūsai, *Tōkokujin michi no ki*, p. 362) ~Kōfu: a castle town in Kai Province (modern-day Yamanashi Prefecture). ~Unsai Sōju: identity unknown. ~This *hokku* was composed during Hideyoshi's campaign in the East Country in 1590.

AUTUMN   (moon) *Nagori aru tsuki ya tomozuna minatofune* (Hosokawa Yūsai, *Kyūshū no michi no ki*, p. 566).

254 *For a 100-verse sequence at the home of Prince Hachijō on the twenty-third day of the Eleventh Month of 1601*

After the white
of morning frost—
falling leaves.

255 *From* Jiteiki

Morning frost
shames snow from falling
on leaves of grass.

Satomura Genjō

256 *Composed on the twelfth day of the Twelfth Month of 1602 for the seventh 100-verse sequence of a 1000-verse memorial event for Jōha*

I lift my gaze
to the summer moon—
and night's no more.

257 *Composed on the twelfth day of the Twelfth Month of 1602 for the third 100-verse sequence of a 1000-verse memorial event for Jōha*

Vying with froth
to be first to vanish—
fireflies.

258 How colorless, now—
fields where I took bush clover
for my garden.

WINTER (frost, falling leaves) *Asashimo no shiroki o nochi no ochiba kana* (Karasumaru Mitsuhiro, *Jiteiki*, p. 194) ~Prince Hachijō: Prince Toshihito (1579–1629), of the Katsuranomiya royal line, who studied poetic lore under Yūsai.

WINTER (frost) *Asashimo no yuki hazukashiki kusaba kana* (Karasumaru Mitsuhiro, *Jiteiki*, p. 157).

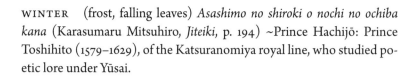

Died 1607. Oldest son of Satomura Jōha (p. 114) and founder of the northern branch of the Satomura lineage of *renga* poets.

SUMMER (summer moon) *Natsu no tsuki furisakemireba yowa mo nashi* (*Hokkuchō*, p. 154).

SUMMER (fireflies) *Mizu no awa ni kie o arasou hotaru kana* (*Hokkuchō*, p. 173).

AUTUMN (bush clover) *Utsushiokite nobe ya iro naki hagi no niwa* (*Hokkuchō*, p. 226).

259 On the river,
a boat bobs on mist—
not water.

260 A gust of wind
sends snow sideways
through the sky.

Matsudaira Ietada

261 *For a 100-verse sequence composed at the home of Atobe of the Ministry of Popular Affairs on the ninth day of the Second Month of 1593, on the felicitous topic "A Tall Plum Tree"*

Green pines.
And among them the red
of a towering plum.

262 *Composed on the last day of the Second Month of 1593, when two 100-verse sequences were composed as a votive offering on behalf of the Major Counselor*

Rising high
to return to earth again—
willow boughs.

263 *For an impromptu gathering at the home of Kyōden on the eighteenth day of the Fifth Month of 1592*

Summer rains:
clouds pile up until—
no more clouds.

AUTUMN   (mist) *Kawafune wa kiri ni ukabite mizu mo nashi* (*Hokkuchō*, p. 235).

WINTER   (snow) *Fukaba sora ni yuki mo katayoru arashi kana* (*Hokkuchō*, p. 355).

Born 1555.   Vassal of Tokugawa Ieyasu (1542–1616), who valued him for his talents as an engineer and a builder; amateur *renga* poet; and patron of Noh drama and the tea ceremony.

SPRING   (plum) *Matsu wa midori ume kurenai no tachie kana* (Matsudaira Ietada, *Ietada nikki*, p. 450) ~Atobe: the Atobe were retainers of the Tokugawa.

SPRING   (willows) *Nabikite no sue wa ne ni kaeru yanagi kana* (Matsudaira Ietada, *Ietada nikki*, p. 452) ~Major Counselor: Tokugawa Ieyasu (1542–1616), founder of the Tokugawa shogunate. ~The taller the willow limb, the more its weight bends it back toward earth.

SUMMER   (summer rains) *Samidare wa kumo kasanarite kumo mo nashi* (Matsudaira Ietada, *Ietada nikki*, p. 425) ~Kyōden: identity unknown. ~The sky is all clouds, and then the rain begins, obscuring all.

264 *Composed for a 100-verse sequence at the home of Shinjirō on the twenty-sixth day of the Twelfth Month of 1590*

Motionless
despite morning wind—
snowy willows.

Shōtaku

265 *Composed at his first meeting in Edo*

Its light
observes no borders—
the moon above.

266 *Composed late in the Genna era (1615–1623)*

Even in snow
the pines stand proper
and straight.

Nishinotō'in Tokiyoshi

267 *Composed on the first day of 1591*

Morning comes—
with last year's snow
just as it was.

WINTER (snow) *Asakaze mo ugokanu yuki no yanagi kana* (Matsudaira Ietada, *Ietada nikki*, p. 381) ~Shinjirō: identity unknown.

Died 1636. A younger son of Satomura Shōshitsu (p. 118) and founder of the southern branch of the Satomura lineage of *renga* poets.

AUTUMN (moon) *Kuniguni no kage kejime nashi sora no tsuki* (Kawazoe, Tanamachi, and Shimazu, eds., *Dazaifu Tenmangū rengashi*, vol. 3, p. 240) ~A celebratory verse. The word *kuniguni*, rendered here as "borders," means literally "the various lands." Since the occasion was the poet's first visit to Edo, the phrase no doubt refers to the many domains of the Tokugawa state.

WINTER (snow) *Yuki ni sae tadashiki matsu no sugata kana* (Kawazoe, Tanamachi, and Shimazu, eds., *Dazaifu Tenmangū rengashi*, vol. 4, p. 64) ~The pine was a common symbol of constancy. Here it quite literally "stands" for correctness and rectitude.

1552–1639. Heir of the Nishinotō'in lineage of the Taira clan, court aristocrat, and *uta* poet.

SPRING (last year's snow) *Kesa ya mata furishi mama naru kozo no yuki* (Nishinotō'in Tokiyoshi, *Tokiyoshi-kyō shū* 363).

268   *Composed on the first day of 1602*

> A new spring day
> marks the halfway-point
> of a hundred years.

269   *Composed in 1605*

> In spring mist
> no mountain is not
> a far mountain.

270   *A hokku composed in 1602 but never used in a meeting*

> Blossoms fall—
> leaving the winds alone
> in the branches.

271   *Composed for the ninth 100-verse sequence of a 1000-verse event held in memory of the late retired emperor at the palace on the twentieth day of the Fourth Month of 1593*

> Light snowflakes fall—
> returning to green
> in the moss below.

Matsunaga Teitoku

272   A sad tale?
       Is that what you want,
       cuckoo?

SPRING (spring day) *Momotose no nakaba koekeri kyō no haru* (Nishinotō'in Tokiyoshi, *Tokiyoshi-kyō shū* 633) ~Tokiyoshi began his fiftieth year in 1602.

SPRING (spring mist) *Kasumu koro tōyama naranu yama mo nashi* (Nishinotō'in Tokiyoshi, *Tokiyoshi-kyō shū* 728).

SPRING (blossoms) *Hana chirite arashi bakari no kozue kana* (Nishinotō'in Tokiyoshi, *Tokiyoshi-kyō shū* 659).

WINTER (snow) *Awayuki wa midori ni kaeru kokeji kana* (Nishinotō'in Tokiyoshi, *Tokiyoshi-kyō shū* 420) ~Late retired emperor: Ōgimachi (1517–1593, r. 1557–1586), who died on the fifth day of the First Month of 1593.

1571–1652. Son of a Nichiren priest; student of Satomura Jōha (p. 114); and professional *renga* master, *uta* poet, *haikai* poet, and scholar.

SUMMER (cuckoo) *Aware naru koto kikasebaya hototogisu* (*Enokoshū* 685).

273 A mountainside—
clad with a sash of clouds
by thunderstorms.

274 In summer heat
we take up fans to fan ourselves—
not the coals.

275 *Composed when someone gave him the topic "Cuckoo in Winter"*

It's still cold,
cuckoo—but,
couldn't you practice?

Wife of Mitsusada

276 Plum branches—
umbrellas taking shape
in spring rain.

277 In the daytime,
where do the fireflies hide?
Pond water.

278 Even your friends
will see only snow—
sleeping crane!

SUMMER   (thunderstorms) *Yama no koshi ni haku yūdachi ya kumo no obi* (*Enokoshū* 893).

SUMMER   (heat, fans) *Natsu no hi wa okosade kiyasu ōgi kana* (*Enokoshū* 915).

WINTER   (cold) *Hototogisu koe tsukae kashi kan no uchi* (*Enokoshū* 1525).

1583–1647.   Wife of Sugiki Mitsusada and often called the first female *haikai* poet.

SPRING   (plum trees) *Umegae wa waga hanakasa ya haru no ame* (*Enokoshū* 148).

SUMMER   (fireflies) *Hotarubi o hiru wa izuku ni ike no mizu* (*Enokoshū* 733).

WINTER   (snow) *Waga tomo o yuki to ya miran sukumisagi* (*Enokoshū* 1417) ~Sleeping crane-style, on one foot and with its head tucked under a wing, the crane becomes invisible in the surrounding snow.

Miura Tamenori

279 *Composed at a meeting where someone had a manuscript in Sōgi's hand*

> The bird flew off
> into the haze—
> but his tracks remain.

280 Clouds disperse
and it no longer moves—
moon in empty sky.

281 Falling onto water,
snow in winter is—
spring snow.

282 *Composed for a sequence offered as a prayer for safe birth*

> Winter branches
> hold in store the hue
> and scent of plum.

Nishiyama Sōin

283 New again, now—
that same old wind
in the willows.

1573–1652. Brother of one of the wives of Tokugawa Ieyasu (1543–1616) and vassal first of Ieyasu and then of his sister's son, Yorinobu (1602–1671).

SPRING   (haze) *Yuku tori no ato wa kasumi o nagori kana* (*Ojinshū*, p. 112) ~Sōgi (p. 58). ~The word *ato* (remains) was used for both tracks and writing.

AUTUMN   (moon) *Kumo harete yuku to wa mienu sora no tsuki* (*Ojinshū*, p. 123).

WINTER   (snow) *Mizu ni furu ya fuyu mo sanagara haru no yuki* (*Ojinshū*, p. 128) ~Even in winter, snow that falls on water quickly melts.

WINTER   (hold in store) *Iro mo ka mo fuyugomoru ume no kozue kana* (*Ojinshū*, p. 128) ~Just as winter confinement will end with plum blossoms, so the poet prays for a happy end to a woman's pregnancy.

1605–1682.   Samurai in service to the Katō clan who became a *renga* master after the forced retirement of his patron, the warlord Katō Masakata (1580–1648), in 1632; student of Shōtaku (p. 130); *renga* steward at Tenmangū Shrine in Osaka, with the support of a newly reinstated Masakata; later turned more to *haikai*, founding what is known as the Danrin school.

SPRING   (willows) *Itsumo fuku kaze atarashiki yanagi kana* (Nishiyama Sōin, *Sōin hokkuchō*, p. 17) ~Every year, the same old wind blows—but always in new spring growth on the willows.

284 Not a wealthy house—
but no less lush
a summer grove.

285 Every year
cicadas sing from higher
in young pines.

286 Lighter
after an evening shower:
summer robe.

287 *Composed for a memorial service*

So far removed
from our dusty world—
cool moon in the sky.

288 Beckoning *me*?
Surely not—
pampas grass.

289 *Composed for a memorial 1000-verse event for Katō Fūan*

On this day,
the time to set forth came—
last fall.

SUMMER (summer grove) *Tomeru ie wa kodachi mo onaji shigeri kana* (Nishiyama Sōin, *Sōin hokkuchō*, p. 43) ~This verse—and most of those by Sōin that follow—reveal a sensibility slightly more plebeian than usually encountered in orthodox *renga*.

SUMMER (cicadas) *Toshidoshi ni semi no ne takashi komatsubara* (Nishiyama Sōin, *Sōin hokkuchō*, p. 59).

SUMMER (summer robe) *Yūdachi ni nurete zo karoki natsugoromo* (Nishiyama Sōin, *Sōin hokkuchō*, p. 62) ~Sweat-soaked before a passing shower, the robe feels lighter after the cleansing rain.

SUMMER (cool) *Yo no chiri o hanarete suzushi sora no tsuki* (Nishiyama Sōin, *Sōin hokkuchō*, p. 63) ~The moon often figures as a metaphor for Buddhist enlightenment.

AUTUMN (pampas grass) *Manekaren ware ka wa ayashi hana susuki* (Nishiyama Sōin, *Sōin hokkuchō*, p. 93) ~Self-deprecating humor? Or perhaps a modern man's statement of alienation from the elegant ways of the past.

AUTUMN (fall) *Tsui ni yuku tsukihi wa kyō ya kozo no aki* (Kawazoe, Tanamachi, and Shimazu, eds., *Dazaifu Tenmangū rengashi*, vol. 2, p. 313) ~Katō Fūan: Katō Masakata, who died on the twenty-third day of the Ninth Month of 1648. ~Compare *KKS* 861, by Ariwara no Narihira (825–880), written when he was ill: Upon this pathway, / I have heard it said, / all set forth at last— / yet I had not thought to go / so soon as today.

290 *Sent to someone who had lost his wife*

"But why now?"
You will ask, awake
in autumn night.

291 Ah, solitude—
it *does* have a color.
Evening showers.

292 Morning showers
letting up at last, I see—
in evening light.

293 *For a sequence held by an elderly man*

In old age—
that's when a snowy pine
looks its best.

294 *Composed for a memorial service for his late wife*

Ah—it was a dream.
How cold is that empty space
in an old man's bed.

AUTUMN   (autumn night) *Toki shimo are omou ran aki no nezame kana*
(Nishiyama Sōin, *Sōin hokkuchō*, p. 123).

WINTER   (showers) *Sabishisa no iro mo arikeri yūshigure* (Nishiyama
Sōin, *Sōin hokkuchō*, p. 125) ~Compare *SKKS* 361, by Jakuren (1139?–
1202): Ah, solitude— / it is not the sort of thing / that has a color. /
Mountains lined with black pine / on an evening in autumn.

WINTER   (showers) *Asashigure haruru to mireba yūhi kana* (Nishiyama
Sōin, *Sōin hokkuchō*, p. 126) ~Winter days are short enough without rainy
skies.

WINTER   (snow) *Oite koso sugata mo masare yuki no matsu* (Nishiyama
Sōin, *Sōin hokkuchō*, p. 146).

WINTER   (cold) *Mishi ya yume katawara samuki oi no toko* (Nishiyama
Sōin, *Sōin hokkuchō*, p. 161).

Nōjun

295 In summer rains
high peaks are buoys
among the clouds.

296 *Composed in the Tenth Month of 1658, when Middle Counselor Toshi-*
tsune passed away

Leaves fall—
but cannot cover
our laments.

297 Fallen on frost
in frost-stricken fields—
leaves of grass.

Konishi Raizan

298 Green, so green—
new greens sprouting
in snowy fields.

299 Glancing back,
I feel the chill of dusk—
in mountain blossoms.

1628–1706.   Son of a priest at Kitano Shrine who became superinten-
dent of Tenjin Shrine in Komatsu, Kaga Province (modern-day Ishikawa
Prefecture), and one of the most prominent *renga* masters of the early
Edo period.

SUMMER   (summer rains) *Samidare wa takane ya kumo no miotsukushi*
(Tsurusaki, *Shirayama manku shiryō to kenkyū*, p. 485).

WINTER   (falling leaves) *Ochiba shite shita ni kakurenu nageki kana*
(Tsurusaki, *Shirayama manku shiryō to kenkyū*, p. 479) ~Middle Coun-
selor Toshitsune: Maeda Toshitsune (1593–1658).

WINTER   (frost, frost-stricken) *Shimogare no shimo ni kakareru kusaba
kana* (Tsurusaki, *Shirayama manku shiryō to kenkyū*, p. 486).

1654–1716.   Native of Osaka and disciple of Nishiyama Sōin (p. 136).

SPRING   (new greens) *Aoshi aoshi wakana wa aoshi yuki no hara* (*Kinsei
haiku haibun shū*, p. 67) ~The repetition of the word "green" qualifies this
verse as *haikai*.

SPRING   (mountain blossoms) *Mikaereba samushi higure no yamazaku-
ra* (*Kinsei haiku haibun shū*, p. 68) ~It is warmer down below by the time
mountain cherry trees bloom, but departing in dusky light the speaker
feels the chill in the mountain air.

300 *"Living Alone"*

I hug my knees—
and feel more keenly
midnight's cold.

Matsuo Bashō

301 *Composed for a duo sequence with Yaba in the spring of 1694*

Fragrance of plum.
Then up pops the sun
on a mountain path.

302 *Composed on the fourth day of the Second Month of 1688 when on pil-*
grimage in Ise

What kind of flower
I don't know, but ah—
such a scent!

303 *Composed in the Second Month of 1688, when he was viewing the blos-*
soms at the villa of Tanganshi and found things there just as they had
been long ago

Ah, the things
they call to mind!
Cherry blossoms.

WINTER   (midnight's cold) *Mi o dakeba mata ikidoshiki yosamu kana* (*Kinsei haiku haibun shū*, p. 70) ~The phrase *mi o daku* (to hug oneself by bringing one's knees up to one's chest) is sufficiently colloquial to qualify this verse, too, as *haikai*, although the somber quality of the scene is more reminiscent of Matsuo Bashō (p. 144) than of earlier *haikai*.

1644–1694.   *Haikai* master and most popular of all *haiku* poets; associated first with the literati poet-scholar Kitamura Kigin (1624–1705) and then with Nishiyama Sōin (p. 136), he went on to form a "school" that would be a major force for generations.

SPRING   (plum) *Mume ga ka ni notto hi no deru yamaji kana* (Kon, *Bashō nenpu taisei* 840) ~Yaba: Shida Yaba (d. 1740), one of the chief disciples of Bashō's last years. ~The eyes of a traveler enjoying the fragrance of plums in the predawn darkness are suddenly drawn along the mountain path to the rising sun.

SPRING   (flower) *Nani no ki no hana to wa shirazu nioi kana* (Kon, *Bashō nenpu taisei* 355) ~Ise: site of the Ise Shrine, dedicated to the Sun Goddess. Bashō was visiting there with one Masumitsu, a shrine official. ~Compare *Sankashū* 2109, attributed to Saigyō (1118–1190), written on a festival day at Ise Shrine: Just what it is / that resides here / I do not know— / but still my eyes overflow / with tears of gratitude.

SPRING   (cherry blossoms) *Samazama no koto omoidasu sakura kana* (Kon, *Bashō nenpu taisei* 367) ~Tanganshi (Tanmaru, d. 1710): son of Tōdō Sengin (d. 1666), to whom Bashō had been in service as a young samurai and who was his first *haikai* teacher. This verse was composed when Bashō was visiting his hometown of Iga Ueno.

304 *Composed on the twenty-seventh day of the Third Month of 1685 at Hōjiji in Atsuta*

Nothing special,
yet even so, enchanting—
wild violets.

305 *Composed for a farewell party at the house of Shisan early in the Fifth Month of 1694*

Hydrangeas—
the start of a garden
for your retreat.

306 *Composed on the twenty-fourth day of the Fifth Month of 1694 at the home of Kakei in Nagoya*

My world—the road.
Back and forth the people go,
paddies to plow.

307 *Composed on the stage of Honma Tanya in Ōtsu in the Sixth Month of 1694*

Fluttering gently
a fan rises into the air.
Pinnacles of cloud.

SPRING   (wild violets) *Nani to wa nashi ni nani yara yukashi sumiregusa* (Kon, *Bashō nenpu taisei* 242) ~Hōjiji: a Sōtō Zen temple, also known as Hakuchōsan, in Atsuta, just outside Nagoya. At the time, Bashō was visiting Hayashi Tōyō (d. 1712), a local innkeeper.

SUMMER   (hydrangeas) *Ajisai ya yabu o koniwa no betsuzashiki* (Kon, *Bashō nenpu taisei* 855) ~Shisan (d. 1699): a resident of Fukagawa in Edo. Bashō left Edo on the eleventh, just a few days after the farewell party, to visit his hometown of Iga Ueno and other points west. ~Bashō suggests that hydrangeas growing in a thicket near his friend's *betsuzashiki* (detached room or small backyard hut) may serve as the beginning of a more formal garden to come.

SUMMER   (paddy plowing) *Yo o tabi ni shiro kaku oda no yukimodori* (Kon, *Bashō nenpu taisei* 866) ~Kakei (d. 1716): a disciple of Bashō who, after Bashō's death, left the world of *haikai* to become a *renga* master, albeit unsuccessfully. ~Bashō contrasts his transient life with the sedentary lives of farmers, although realizing that at planting time they, too, are "on the road."

SUMMER   (fan) *Hirahira to aguru ōgi ya kumo no mine* (Kon, *Bashō nenpu taisei* 881) ~Honma Tanya: a Noh dramatist. Bashō, Tanya, and four others composed a short sequence of thirteen verses on the drama troupe's *butai* (stage). ~Ōtsu: a city on the southern tip of Lake Biwa. ~Noh artists often use fans in performance.

308　*Composed on the eighth day of the Seventh Month of 1688 at the home of Chisoku, in celebration of the new dwelling of the latter's younger brother, Chishi*

A fine house!
Sparrows love the millet
'round back.

309　*On the topic "Looking Out on the Vista at Narumi," composed for a session held by Jūshin on the tenth day of the Seventh Month of 1688*

Autumn begins:
the sea, the paddies,
all green.

310　*Composed in Kyoto late in the Seventh Month of 1691*

In the cowshed,
mosquito voices, failing.
Autumn wind.

311　*Composed after the fifteenth day of the Eighth Month of 1690 for a duo sequence with Shōhaku at Gichūji in Ōtsu*

Moon viewing.
Not a handsome face
in the room.

312　*Composed at the home of Narihide in Katada on the sixteenth day of the Eighth Month of 1691*

So willing at first—
now the moon hangs back
in the clouds.

AUTUMN   (millet) *Yoki ie ya suzume yorokobu sedo no awa* (Kon, *Bashō nenpu taisei* 433) ~Chisoku (1640–1704): a *haikai* enthusiast who was in the *saké* business in Narumi, near Nagoya.

AUTUMN   *Hatsuaki ya umi yara ta yara midori kana* (Kon, *Bashō nenpu taisei* 434) ~Jūshin (d. 1727): a warehouseman in Narumi. Also attending the meeting, held just two days after the one noted in poem 308, were local *haikai* enthusiasts Chisoku and Jishō (p. 153).

AUTUMN   (autumn wind) *Ushibeya ni ka no koe yowashi aki no kaze* (Kon, *Bashō nenpu taisei* 705).

AUTUMN   (moon) *Tsukimi suru za ni utsukushiki kao mo nashi* (Kon, *Bashō nenpu taisei* 649) ~Shōhaku: Esa Shōhaku (1650–1722), a physician in Ōtsu and disciple of Bashō. ~Gichūji: a Tendai temple in Ōtsu, where Bashō often stayed in a cottage called Mumyōan (Nameless Hut).

AUTUMN   (moon) *Yasuyasu to idete izayou tsuki no kumo* (Kon, *Bashō nenpu taisei* 712) ~Narihide: Takeuchi Narihide, a local disciple of Bashō. ~Katada: a city on the western shore of Lake Biwa. Bashō and some companions traveled there by boat from where he was staying at Mumyōan in Ōtsu, to be feted by Narihide.

313 *Composed at the house of Shayō on the twenty-first day of the Ninth Month of 1694, when rain had fallen ceaselessly for two days*

To break the tedium
of an autumn night—
we share stories.

314 *Sent to Shihaku on the twenty-eighth day of the Ninth Month of 1694, for a meeting to be held the next night at the latter's house*

Autumn wanes.
That man next door—
what is it he does?

315 *Composed in the Eleventh Month of 1684 at the home of Tōyō in Atsuta*

Into the sea
I'll cast my sandals,
my hat—rain and all.

316 *Composed late in the Tenth Month of 1691, at the house of Baijin in Atsuta*

Narcissus
reflected by a paper door:
white on white.

AUTUMN (autumn night) *Aki no yo o uchi kuzushitaru hanashi kana* (Kon, *Bashō nenpu taisei* 914) ~Shayō: Shioe Shayō, a disciple of Bashō from Osaka.

AUTUMN *Aki fukaki tonari wa nani o suru hito zo* (Kon, *Bashō nenpu taisei* 923) ~Shihaku: Negoro Shihaku (1643–1713). ~Bashō was too ill to attend the meeting. This *hokku* was the last one Bashō wrote for an actual sequence. He died two weeks later.

WINTER (rain) *Kono umi ni waranji suten kasashigure* (Kon, *Bashō nenpu taisei* 217) ~Tōyō: Hayashi Tōyō (p. 147). ~Bashō had arrived in Atsuta from Ise, by way of Kuwana—on foot, of course. No doubt, his sandals and rain hat were ready to be cast off.

WINTER (narcissus) *Suisen ya shiroki shōji no tomo utsuri* (Kon, *Bashō nenpu taisei* 737) ~Baijin: the owner of the Ebisuya, the inn where Bashō was staying at the time. ~The white of narcissus flowers is intensified against the white of a sliding paper door.

317 *Composed at the house of Ryōbon on the first day of the Eleventh Month of 1689*

Come on, kids!
Let's have ourselves a run
among the hailstones.

318 *Composed at the home of Bokugen in Narumi on the fifth day of the Eleventh Month of 1687*

Today, only halfway
to the capital, and yet—
snow clouds.

319 *Composed at the house of Jishō in Narumi on the twentieth day of the Eleventh Month of 1687*

Now, *this* I like:
snowflakes starting to form
in winter rain.

320 *Composed on the fourth day of the Twelfth Month of 1687 for a sequence composed at the home of Minoya Chōsetsu in Atsuta*

Up ahead, someone
will be at Hakone.
Morning snow.

WINTER   (hail) *Iza kodomo hashiriarikan tamaarare* (Kon, *Bashō nenpu taisei* 592) ~Ryōbon: Tomoda Ryōbon (d. 1730), a samurai in service to the Tōdō clan in Iga Ueno, Bashō's hometown.

WINTER   (snow clouds) *Kyō made wa mada nakazora ya yuki no kumo* (Kon, *Bashō nenpu taisei* 323) ~Bokugen: Terashima Bokugen (d. 1736), the brother-in-law of Chisoku (p. 149). ~Bashō alludes here to an *uta* composed by Asukai Masaaki (d. 1679) on a visit to Narumi: Today, I arrive / at last on the shores / of Narumi— / come from far Kyoto, / out across the vast sea.

WINTER   (snow) *Omoshiroshi yuki ni ya naran fuyu no ame* (Kon, *Bashō nenpu taisei* 336) ~Jishō: Okajima Jishō (d. 1713), a swordsmith in Narumi. ~Rain gets boring after a while—but when snowflakes start to appear, things become more interesting.

WINTER   (snow) *Hakone kosu hito mo aru rashi kesa no yuki* (Kon, *Bashō nenpu taisei* 341) ~Minoya Chōsetsu: most likely, a man of the merchant class. ~Hakone: the pass through the mountains around Mount Fuji that is the gateway to Edo and the East Country. ~Footprints in the morning snow remind the poet that other travelers are laboring through the snow while he enjoys the hospitality of his host.

Bibliography

The following abbreviations refer to sources frequently cited.

FGS	*Fūgashū*. In SKT.
GSIS	*Goshūishū*. In SKT.
GSS	*Gosenshū*. In SKT.
KB	Koten bunko. 541 vols. Tokyo: Koten bunko, 1946–.
KKS	*Kokinshū*. In SKT.
NKBT	Nihon koten bungaku taikei. 102 vols. Tokyo: Iwanami shoten, 1956–1968.
NKBZ	Nihon koten bungaku zenshū. 60 vols. Tokyo: Shōgakkan, 1970–1976.
NKT	Nihon kagaku taikei. 10 vols., 5 supplementary vols. Tokyo: Kazama shobō, 1977–1981.
SCSS	*Shin chokusenshū*. In SKT.
ShokuGSS	*Shoku gosenshū*. In SKT.
ShokuKKS	*Shoku kokinshū*. In SKT.
SIS	*Shūishū*. In SKT.
SKKS	*Shin kokinshū*. In SKT.
SKS	*Shikashū*. In SKT.
SKT	Shinpen kokka taikan. 10 vols. Tokyo: Kadokawa shoten, 1983–1992.
SNKBT	Shin Nihon koten bungaku taikei. 100 vols., 5 supplementary vols. Tokyo: Iwanami shoten, 1989–.

SNKBZ   Shin Nihon koten bungaku zenshū. Tokyo: Shōgakkan, 1994–.
ST   Shikashū taisei. 8 vols. Tokyo: Meiji shoin, 1973–1976.
SZS   *Senzaishū.* In SKT.
ZGR   Zoku gunsho ruijū. 33 vols. Tokyo: Zoku gunsho ruijū kansei-
         kai, 1957–1975.

Chikurinshō. Edited by Shimazu Tadao et al. SNKBT, vol. 49.

Chiun. *Chikamasa kushū.* In *Shichiken jidai renga kushū,* edited by Kaneko Kinjirō and Ōta Takeo. Tokyo: Kadokawa shoten, 1978.

Enokoshū. In *Shoki haikai shū,* edited by Katō Sadahiko and Morikawa Akira. SNKBT, vol. 69.

Fushiminomiya Sadafusa. *Kanmon nikki.* 2 vols. Tokyo: Zoku gunsho ruijū kanseikai, 1958, 1959.

Fushiminomiya Sadafusa. *Kanmon nikki shihai monjo.* In *Kanmon nikki shihai monjo, bekki,* edited by Kunaichō Shoryōbu. Nara: Yōtokusha, 1965.

Gyōjo. *Gyōjo kushū.* In *Shichiken jidai renga kushū,* edited by Kaneko Kinjirō and Ōta Takeo. Tokyo: Kadokawa shoten, 1978.

Hokkuchō. Edited by Morikawa Akira. KB, vol. 456.

Hokku kikigaki. In *Renga to chūsei bungei,* edited by Kaneko Kinjirō. Kaneko Kinjirō Hakase Koki Kinen Ronshū Henshū Iinkai. Tokyo: Kadokawa shoten, 1977.

Hōraku hokku shū (Jingū Bunko-bon). International Research Center for Japanese Studies. http://tois.nichibun.ac.jp/database/html2/renga/renga_i869.html.

Hosokawa Yūsai. *Kyūshū no michi no ki.* Edited by Itō Kei. In *Chūsei nikki kikō shū.* SNKBZ, vol. 48.

Hosokawa Yūsai. *Tōkokujin michi no ki.* In Hosokawa Morisada, *Hosokawa Yūsai.* Tokyo: Chūō kōronsha, 1994.

Ikkadō Jōa. *Sekitai.* In Tsurusaki Hiro, *Sengoku no kenryoku to yoriai no bungei.* Tokyo: Izumi shoin, 1988.

Inawashiro Kensai. *Sono no chiri.* In ZGR, vol. 17.

Ishiyama hyakuin. In ZGR, vol. 17.

Kabegusachū. In *Renga kochūshaku shū,* edited by Kaneko Kinjirō. Tokyo: Kadokawa shoten, 1979.

Kaneko Kinjirō. *Rengashi Kensai denkō.* Tokyo: Ōfūsha, 1962.

Karasumaru Mitsuhiro. *Jiteiki.* In NKT, vol. 6.

Kawazoe Shōji, Tanamachi Tomoya, and Shimazu Tadao, eds. *Dazaifu Tenmangū rengashi: shiryō to kenkyū.* Vols. 2–4. Fukuoka: Tenmangū bunka kenkyūjo, 1981.

Kensai zōdan. In NKT, vol. 5.

Kidō Saizō. *Rengashi ronkō.* 2 vols. Tokyo: Meiji shoin, 1971, 1973.

Kinsei haiku haibun shū. Edited by Abe Kimio and Asō Isoji. NKBT, vol. 92.

Kon Eizō. *Bashō nenpu taisei.* Tokyo: Kadokawa shoten, 1991.

Matsudaira Ietada. *Ietada nikki.* Edited by Takeuchi Rizō. Zoku shiryō taisei, vol. 20. 2 vols. Kyoto: Rinsen shoten, 1967.

Murasaki Shikibu. *The Tale of Genji.* Translated by Edward Seidensticker. 2 vols. New York: Knopf, 1976.

Nijō Yoshimoto. *Tsukuba mondō.* In *Haironshū, rengaronshū, nōgaku ronshū.* In NKBT, vol. 66.

Nikonshū. 2 vols. KB, vols. 335, 343.

Nishinotō'in Tokiyoshi. *Tokiyoshi-kyō shū.* In ST, vol. 5.

Nishiyama Sōin. *Sōin hokkuchō.* In *Haisho sōkan,* edited by Tenri Toshokan Wataya Bunko. Vol. 1. Kyoto: Rinsen shoten, 1988.

Ojinshū. In *Haisho sōkan,* edited by Tenri Toshokan Wataya Bunko. Vol. 1. Kyoto: Rinsen shoten, 1988.

Oka Kōsetsu. *Kōsetsu eisō.* In ST, vol. 5.

Ōtabon Shunmusōchū. In *Renga kochūshaku shū,* edited by Kaneko Kinjirō. Tokyo: Kadokawa shoten, 1979.

Reizei Tamekazu. *Tamekazu shū.* In ST, vol. 5.

Saigyō. *Sankashū.* In SKT, vol. 3.

Sakurai Motosuke. *Sakurai Motosuke shū.* KB, vol. 586.

Sanjōnishi Sanetaka. *Saishōsō.* In ST, vol. 5, part 1.

Sanjōnishi Sanetaka. *Saishōsō* addendum. In ST, vol. 5, part 2.

Sanjōnishi Sanetaka. *Sanetaka-kō ki.* Edited by Takahashi Ryūzō. 14 vols. Tokyo: Zoku gunsho ruijū kanseikai, 1931–1963.

Satomura Jōha. *Jōha hokkuchō.* In Morozumi Sōichi, *Rengashi Jōha: denki to hokkuchō.* Tokyo: Shintensha, 2002.

Satomura Jōha and Satomura Shōshitsu. *Mōri senku.* In *Renga kochūshaku no kenkyū,* edited by Kaneko Kinjirō. Tokyo: Kadokawa shoten, 1974.

Senjun. *Hōgen Senjun kushū.* In *Shichiken jidai renga kushū,* edited by Kaneko Kinjirō and Ōta Takeo. Tokyo: Kadokawa shoten, 1978.

Shinkei. *Shibakusa kunai hokku.* In *Shinkei sakuhin shū,* edited by Yokoyama Shigeru. Tokyo: Kadokawa shoten, 1972.

Shinkei. *Shingyoku shūi.* In *Shinkei sakuhin shū,* edited by Yokoyama Shigeru. Tokyo: Kadokawa shoten, 1972.

Shinkei. *Tokorodokoro hentō.* In *Rengaronshū,* edited by Kidō Saizō and Shigematsu Hiromi. Vol. 3. Tokyo: Miyai shoten, 1985.

Shinsen Tsukubashū (Sanetaka-bon). Edited by Kaneko Kinjirō and Yokoyama Shigeru. Tokyo: Kadokawa shoten, 1978.

Shōji shodo hyakushu. In SKT, vol. 4.

Sōchō. *Kabekusa.* KB, vol. 424.

Sōchō. *Nachigomori.* KB, vol. 376.

Sōchō. *Sōchō shuki.* In *Sōchō nikki*, edited by Shimazu Tadao. Iwanami bunko. Tokyo: Iwanami shoten, 1975.

Sōchō and Sōseki. *Ise senku.* In *Renga kochūshaku no kenkyū*, edited by Kaneko Kinjirō. Tokyo: Kadokawa shoten, 1974.

Sōgi. *Azuma mondō.* In *Renga haikai shū.* NKBT, vol. 66.

Sōgi. *Jinensai hokku.* In *Sōgi hokku shū*, edited by Hoshika Sōichi. Iwanami bunko. Tokyo: Iwanami shoten, 1953.

Sōgi. *Wakuraba.* In *Sōgi kushū*, edited by Ijichi Tetsuo and Kaneko Kinjirō. Tokyo: Kadokawa shoten, 1977.

Takayama Sōzei. *Kokon rendanshū.* In *Rengaronshū*, edited by Ikeda Shigeru. KB, vol. 85.

Takayama Sōzei. *Mitsudenshō.* In *Rengaronshū*, edited by Kidō Saizō and Shigematsu Hiromi. Vol. 3. Tokyo: Miyai shoten, 1985.

Takayama Sōzei. *Shoshin kyūeishū.* In *Rengaronshū*, edited by Kidō Saizō and Shigematsu Hiromi. Vol. 3. Tokyo: Miyai shoten, 1985.

Takayama Sōzei. *Sōzei hokku narabi ni tsukeku nukigaki.* In *Shichiken jidai renga kushū*, edited by Kaneko Kinjirō and Ōta Takeo. Tokyo: Kadokawa shoten, 1978.

Takayama Sōzei. *Sōzei ku.* In *Shichiken jidai renga kushū*, edited by Kaneko Kinjirō and Ōta Takeo. Tokyo: Kadokawa shoten, 1978.

Takayama Sōzei. *Zeikahokku.* In *Shichiken jidai renga kushū*, edited by Kaneko Kinjirō and Ōta Takeo. Tokyo: Kadokawa shoten, 1978.

Tani Sōboku. *Kanazawa kushū.* In Ogawa Kōzō, "*Sōboku Tōkoku kikō hotei.*" In *Renga kenkyū no tenkai*, edited by Kaneko Kinjirō. Tokyo: Benseisha, 1985.

Tani Sōboku. *Kochiku.* In *Renga kochūshaku shū*, edited by Kaneko Kinjirō. Tokyo: Kadokawa shoten, 1979.

Tonna. *Seiashō.* In NKT, vol. 5.

Tsukubashū. Edited by Fukui Kyūzō. 2 vols. Nihon koten zensho, vol. 69. Tokyo: Asahi Shinbunsha, 1948, 1951.

Tsurusaki Hirō. *Shirayama manku shiryō to kenkyū.* Hakusan: Shirayama Hime Jinja, 1985.

Asian Classics

Major Plays of Chikamatsu, tr. Donald Keene 1961

Four Major Plays of Chikamatsu, tr. Donald Keene. Paperback ed. only. 1961; rev. ed. 1997

Records of the Grand Historian of China, translated from the Shih chi of Ssu-ma Ch'ien, tr. Burton Watson, 2 vols. 1961

Instructions for Practical Living and Other Neo-Confucian Writings by Wang Yang-ming, tr. Wing-tsit Chan 1963

Hsün Tzu: Basic Writings, tr. Burton Watson, paperback ed. only. 1963; rev. ed. 1996

Chuang Tzu: Basic Writings, tr. Burton Watson, paperback ed. only. 1964; rev. ed. 1996

The Mahābhārata, tr. Chakravarthi V. Narasimhan. Also in paperback ed. 1965; rev. ed. 1997

The Manyōshū, Nippon Gakujutsu Shinkōkai edition 1965

Su Tung-p'o: Selections from a Sung Dynasty Poet, tr. Burton Watson. Also in paperback ed. 1965

Bhartrihari: Poems, tr. Barbara Stoler Miller. Also in paperback ed. 1967

Basic Writings of Mo Tzu, Hsün Tzu, and Han Fei Tzu, tr. Burton Watson. Also in separate paperback eds. 1967

The Awakening of Faith, Attributed to Aśvaghosha, tr. Yoshito S. Hakeda. Also in paperback ed. 1967

Reflections on Things at Hand: The Neo-Confucian Anthology, comp. Chu Hsi and Lü Tsu-ch'ien, tr. Wing-tsit Chan 1967

The Platform Sutra of the Sixth Patriarch, tr. Philip B. Yampolsky. Also in paperback ed. 1967

Essays in Idleness: The Tsurezuregusa of Kenkō, tr. Donald Keene. Also in paperback ed. 1967

The Pillow Book of Sei Shōnagon, tr. Ivan Morris, 2 vols. 1967

Two Plays of Ancient India: The Little Clay Cart and the Minister's Seal, tr. J. A. B. van Buitenen 1968

The Complete Works of Chuang Tzu, tr. Burton Watson 1968

The Romance of the Western Chamber (Hsi Hsiang chi), tr. S. I. Hsiung. Also in paperback ed. 1968

The Manyōshū, Nippon Gakujutsu Shinkōkai edition. Paperback ed. only. 1969

Records of the Historian: Chapters from the Shih chi of Ssu-ma Ch'ien, tr. Burton Watson. Paperback ed. only. 1969

Cold Mountain: 100 Poems by the T'ang Poet Han-shan, tr. Burton Watson. Also in paperback ed. 1970

Twenty Plays of the Nō Theatre, ed. Donald Keene. Also in paperback ed. 1970

Chūshingura: The Treasury of Loyal Retainers, tr. Donald Keene. Also in paperback ed. 1971; rev. ed. 1997

The Zen Master Hakuin: Selected Writings, tr. Philip B. Yampolsky 1971

Chinese Rhyme-Prose: Poems in the Fu Form from the Han and Six Dynasties Periods, tr. Burton Watson. Also in paperback ed. 1971

Kūkai: Major Works, tr. Yoshito S. Hakeda. Also in paperback ed. 1972

The Old Man Who Does as He Pleases: Selections from the Poetry and Prose of Lu Yu, tr. Burton Watson 1973

The Lion's Roar of Queen Śrīmālā, tr. Alex and Hideko Wayman 1974

Courtier and Commoner in Ancient China: Selections from the History of the Former Han by Pan Ku, tr. Burton Watson. Also in paperback ed. 1974

Japanese Literature in Chinese, vol. 1: Poetry and Prose in Chinese by Japanese Writers of the Early Period, tr. Burton Watson 1975

Japanese Literature in Chinese, vol. 2: Poetry and Prose in Chinese by Japanese Writers of the Later Period, tr. Burton Watson 1976

Love Song of the Dark Lord: Jayadeva's Gītagovinda, tr. Barbara Stoler Miller. Also in paperback ed. Cloth ed. includes critical text of the Sanskrit. 1977; rev. ed. 1997

Ryōkan: Zen Monk-Poet of Japan, tr. Burton Watson 1977

Calming the Mind and Discerning the Real: From the Lam rim chen mo of Tsoṇ-kha-pa, tr. Alex Wayman 1978

The Hermit and the Love-Thief: Sanskrit Poems of Bhartrihari and Bilhaṇa, tr. Barbara Stoler Miller 1978

The Lute: Kao Ming's P'i-p'a chi, tr. Jean Mulligan. Also in paperback ed. 1980

A Chronicle of Gods and Sovereigns: Jinnō Shōtōki of Kitabatake Chikafusa, tr. H. Paul Varley 1980

Among the Flowers: The Hua-chien chi, tr. Lois Fusek 1982

Grass Hill: Poems and Prose by the Japanese Monk Gensei, tr. Burton Watson 1983

Doctors, Diviners, and Magicians of Ancient China: Biographies of Fang-shih, tr. Kenneth J. DeWoskin. Also in paperback ed. 1983

Theater of Memory: The Plays of Kālidāsa, ed. Barbara Stoler Miller. Also in paperback ed. 1984

The Columbia Book of Chinese Poetry: From Early Times to the Thirteenth Century, ed. and tr. Burton Watson. Also in paperback ed. 1984

Poems of Love and War: From the Eight Anthologies and the Ten Long Poems of Classical Tamil, tr. A. K. Ramanujan. Also in paperback ed. 1985

The Bhagavad Gita: Krishna's Counsel in Time of War, tr. Barbara Stoler Miller 1986

The Columbia Book of Later Chinese Poetry, ed. and tr. Jonathan Chaves. Also in paperback ed. 1986

The Tso Chuan: Selections from China's Oldest Narrative History, tr. Burton Watson 1989

Waiting for the Wind: Thirty-six Poets of Japan's Late Medieval Age, tr. Steven Carter 1989

Selected Writings of Nichiren, ed. Philip B. Yampolsky 1990

Saigyō, Poems of a Mountain Home, tr. Burton Watson 1990

The Book of Lieh Tzu: A Classic of the Tao, tr. A. C. Graham. Morningside ed. 1990

The Tale of an Anklet: An Epic of South India—The Cilappatikāram of Ilaṅkō Aṭikaḷ, tr. R. Parthasarathy 1993

Waiting for the Dawn: A Plan for the Prince, tr. with introduction by Wm. Theodore de Bary 1993

Yoshitsune and the Thousand Cherry Trees: A Masterpiece of the Eighteenth-Century Japanese Puppet Theater, tr., annotated, and with introduction by Stanleigh H. Jones, Jr. 1993

The Lotus Sutra, tr. Burton Watson. Also in paperback ed. 1993

The Classic of Changes: A New Translation of the I Ching as Interpreted by Wang Bi, tr. Richard John Lynn 1994

Beyond Spring: Tz'u Poems of the Sung Dynasty, tr. Julie Landau 1994

The Columbia Anthology of Traditional Chinese Literature, ed. Victor H. Mair 1994

Scenes for Mandarins: The Elite Theater of the Ming, tr. Cyril Birch 1995

Letters of Nichiren, ed. Philip B. Yampolsky; tr. Burton Watson et al. 1996

Unforgotten Dreams: Poems by the Zen Monk Shōtetsu, tr. Steven D. Carter 1997

The Vimalakirti Sutra, tr. Burton Watson 1997

Japanese and Chinese Poems to Sing: The Wakan rōei shū, tr. J. Thomas Rimer and Jonathan Chaves 1997

Breeze Through Bamboo: Kanshi of Ema Saikō, tr. Hiroaki Sato 1998

A Tower for the Summer Heat, by Li Yu, tr. Patrick Hanan 1998

Traditional Japanese Theater: An Anthology of Plays, by Karen Brazell 1998

The Original Analects: Sayings of Confucius and His Successors (0479–0249), by E. Bruce Brooks and A. Taeko Brooks 1998

The Classic of the Way and Virtue: A New Translation of the Tao-te ching *of Laozi as Interpreted by Wang Bi*, tr. Richard John Lynn 1999

The Four Hundred Songs of War and Wisdom: An Anthology of Poems from Classical Tamil, The Puṟanāṉūṟu, ed. and tr. George L. Hart and Hank Heifetz 1999

Original Tao: Inward Training (Nei-yeh) *and the Foundations of Taoist Mysticism*, by Harold D. Roth 1999

Lao Tzu's Tao Te Ching: *A Translation of the Startling New Documents Found at Guodian*, by Robert G. Henricks 2000

The Shorter Columbia Anthology of Traditional Chinese Literature, ed. Victor H. Mair 2000

Mistress and Maid (Jiaohongji), by Meng Chengshun, tr. Cyril Birch 2001

Chikamatsu: Five Late Plays, tr. and ed. C. Andrew Gerstle 2001

The Essential Lotus: Selections from the Lotus Sutra, tr. Burton Watson 2002

Early Modern Japanese Literature: An Anthology, 1600–1900, ed. Haruo Shirane 2002; abridged 2008

The Columbia Anthology of Traditional Korean Poetry, ed. Peter H. Lee 2002

The Sound of the Kiss, or The Story That Must Never Be Told: Pingali Suranna's Kalapurnodayamu, tr. Vecheru Narayana Rao and David Shulman 2003

The Selected Poems of Du Fu, tr. Burton Watson 2003

Far Beyond the Field: Haiku by Japanese Women, tr. Makoto Ueda 2003

Just Living: Poems and Prose by the Japanese Monk Tonna, ed. and tr. Steven D. Carter 2003

Han Feizi: Basic Writings, tr. Burton Watson 2003

Mozi: Basic Writings, tr. Burton Watson 2003

Xunzi: Basic Writings, tr. Burton Watson 2003

Zhuangzi: Basic Writings, tr. Burton Watson 2003

The Awakening of Faith, Attributed to Aśvaghosha, tr. Yoshito S. Hakeda, introduction by Ryuichi Abe 2005

The Tales of the Heike, tr. Burton Watson, ed. Haruo Shirane 2006

Tales of Moonlight and Rain, by Ueda Akinari, tr. with introduction by Anthony H. Chambers 2007

Traditional Japanese Literature: An Anthology, Beginnings to 1600, ed. Haruo Shirane 2007

The Philosophy of Qi, by Kaibara Ekken, tr. Mary Evelyn Tucker 2007

The Analects of Confucius, tr. Burton Watson 2007

The Art of War: Sun Zi's Military Methods, tr. Victor Mair 2007

One Hundred Poets: One Poem Each: A Translation of the Ogura Hyakunin Isshu, tr. Peter McMillan 2008

Zeami: Performance Notes, tr. Tom Hare 2008

Zongmi on Chan, tr. Jeffrey Lyle Broughton 2009

Scripture of the Lotus Blossom of the Fine Dharma, rev. ed., tr. Leon Hurvitz, preface and introduction by Stephen R. Teiser 2009

Mencius, tr. Irene Bloom, ed. with an introduction by Philip J. Ivanhoe 2009

Clouds Thick, Whereabouts Unknown: Poems by Zen Monks of China, Charles Egan 2010

The Mozi: A Complete Translation, tr. Ian Johnston 2010

The Huainanzi: A Guide to the Theory and Practice of Government in Early Han China, by Liu An, tr. John S. Major, Sarah A. Queen, Andrew Seth Meyer, and Harold D. Roth, with Michael Puett and Judson Murray 2010

The Demon at Agi Bridge and Other Japanese Tales, tr. Burton Watson, ed. with introduction by Haruo Shirane 2011